Contents

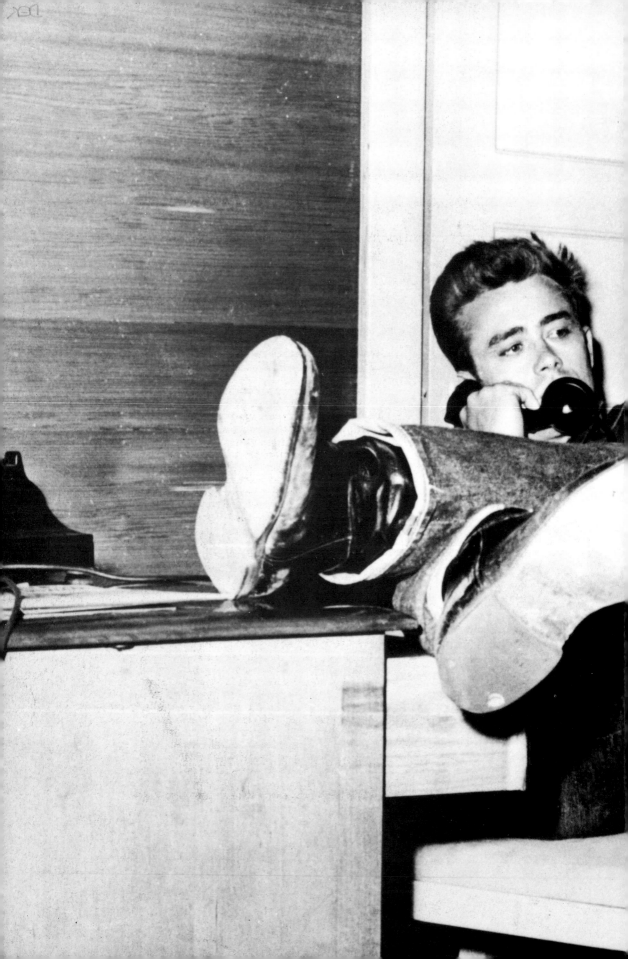

James Dean In His Own Words

"America has known many rebellions — but *none* like this. Millions of teenage rebels heading for nowhere: some in hot rod cars, others on the blare of rock 'n' roll music, some with guns in their hands. And at their head a dead leader."

So trumpeted the *Picture Post* in 1956, fearlessly pioneering the art of tabloid journalism . . . yet accurately reflecting the fear engendered by a star whose fan following actually *grew* after his death.

The cult Dean's demise inspired took the name 'Deanagers' . . . and attracted the scorn, derision and, yes, *fear* of the older generation. No matter that teen idols had always come in suits: the fact was this idol was dead. And with no known or documented resurrection, worship was deemed totally sacrilegious . . . Add the well-known 'crucifixion' pose from the *Giant* publicity shot, stir in a suspicion of suicide . . . and you have a combustible mixture that approaches blasphemy.

Thirty-three years on, much mystery remains. Dean's death itself — was it really an accident? Then there's Dean's sexuality, of which more later. Yet perhaps the greatest mystery is how Dean's legend has lasted 10 times longer than his major movie career.

Much of this has to do with the image. Musicians need a sound to complete the whole picture. But a shot of Dean in typically sullen, rebellious pose strikes a universal chord. "A curious case of juvenile frustration, sex-substitution and hero-worship running like electrical lines into a centrally convenient fuse box," was one psychologist's verdict. What he would have made of Elvis, The Beatles, Wham! or Bros remains unrecorded. But Dean was the first — and like Buddy Holly he was cut down before he had time to blot his copybook, sell out or conform. Not that Dean showed any sign of doing *that* . . .

What made James Dean the man he was? Much has been made of Dean's loss of his mother at an early age: he himself referred to it many times in his adult life. He was certainly far from lucky in love. Italian actress Pier Angeli, by all accounts the great love of his life, jilted him to marry singer Vic Damone: Dean sat opposite the church on a motorcycle, roaring angrily away as the happy couple emerged.

A strong undercurrent of rumour exists today suggesting that Dean was gay or at best bisexual: foundation for this ranges from a supposed 'constellation' of cigarette burns found on the corpse, to his alleged confession to escape National Service. Then again, if half the number of alleged affairs (of *any* nature) Dean had in his short life were true, he'd have been hard-pressed to leave the bedroom long enough to make even three films. On the contrary, those close to him suggested that his passion was reserved for his work.

Dean's name has cropped up many times as a rock 'n' roll icon. The Eagles, David Essex and many more have deified him in song — countless others have cashed in on his image. So was James Dean the first rock 'n' roll star? The question isn't quite as silly as it at first sounds.

The uniform Dean adopted proved enduring: jeans and a white T-shirt, the garb he employed even at press conferences. Levi's should have paid him a royalty.

Suddenly every rock group had its Dean. The Beatles' Dean was of course Stuart Sutcliffe, The Stones' Brian Jones one supposes. Elvis was impressed enough to admit to knowing all Dean's movie dialogue backwards. If parental disapproval was anything to go by, he had Johnny Rotten beaten out of sight.

James Dean In His Own Words is in many ways a contradiction in terms. The look, of course, was everything. Dean didn't say much, and most of what he did say was mumbled, Brando-style — a trait even his devoted agent, Jane Deacy, bawled him out for on at least one occasion. His dialogue in the films only helped to fuel the myth: his stereotype was the rebel, the misunderstood . . .

The great majority of what Dean *did* say is here. The remainder is made up of first-hand contemporary comment — and with reason. If Dean's myth flowered in the years after his death, then only those who were there in life can give anything approaching the unvarnished truth about the man. Painstaking months of research reveal no substitute.

His image may live on — but few conventional monuments (save his constantly defaced gravestone in Fairmount, Indiana) remain to the man. A James Dean Foundation in New York providing scholarships for young actors flopped soon after it started, while the Dean Foundation in Fairmount lasted only a few years. Significantly, neither institution attracted financial support from the likes of Warner Brothers, who showed no such reticence in raking in the proceeds from *Giant*, the posthumously released finale to Dean's brief, glorious career.

As for awards, these were few — a posthumous Academy Award nomination to add to recognition for the stage play *The Immoralist*. Ironically, at the time of his death, Dean was slated to play in *Somebody Up There Likes Me*. Most of his work was for that critically unloved medium, television: his last small-screen work was the Schlitz playhouse drama *The Unlighted Road*, broadcast on May 6, 1955 — the week filming started on his last picture.

If you bought this book expecting a conclusive verdict on Dean, you'll be sadly disappointed. But all the evidence — from Dean himself and those who knew him best — is here, even if it often conflicts wildly. Henry Ginsburg, the producer of *Giant*, said: "In 16 months of acting he left more of a lasting impression on the public than many stars do in 30 years."

George Stevens, his director, didn't agree. "A few more films," he growled, "and the fans wouldn't have been so bereft."

If those he worked with can have such contrary opinions, then what chance have we three decades later? Read what Dean — and his closest colleagues — had to say. The verdict, then, is yours alone.

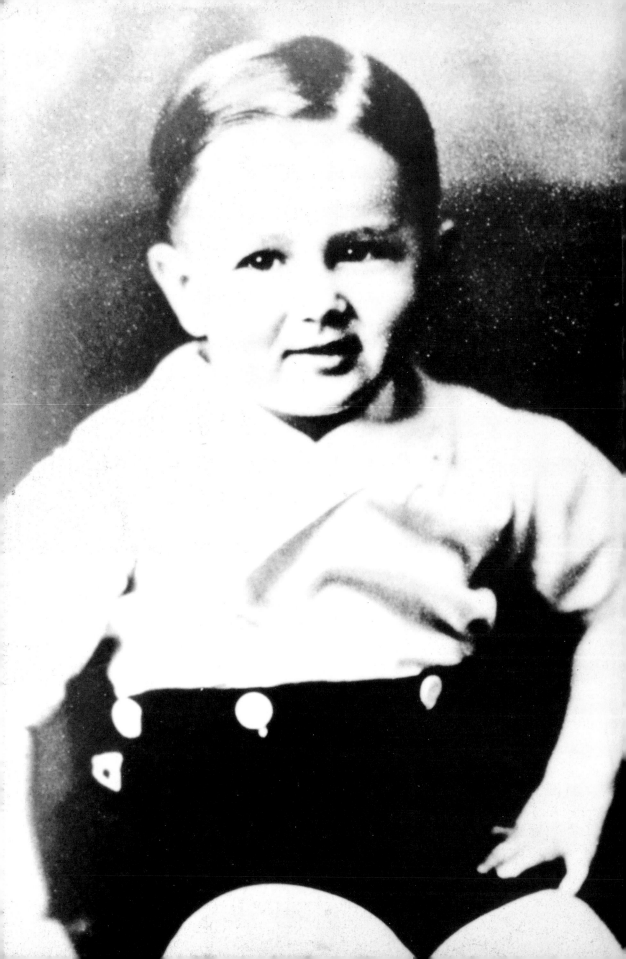

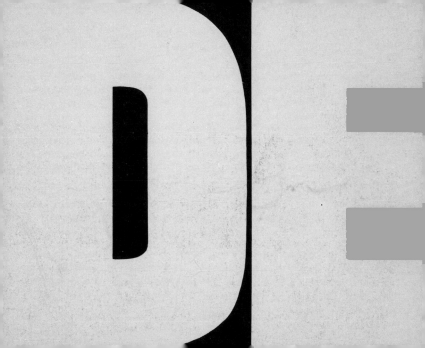

James Dean In His Own Words

"She was only 29. The doctors told me it was hopeless. How do you tell an eight-year-old boy his mother's going to die? I tried, but I just couldn't make it. Jim and I — we've never had that closeness. And my Jim is a tough boy to understand."
FATHER WINTON DEAN.

"Nowadays he lives in a world we don't understand too well — the actors' world. We don't see too much of him. But he's a good boy, my Jim. A good boy, and I'm very proud of him. Not easy to understand. No sir. But he's all man, and he'll make his mark. Mind you, my boy will make his mark."
FATHER WINTON DEAN.

"Everything's so artificial here. I want my son to grow up where things are real and simple."
MILDRED DEAN IN CALIFORNIA TO VISITING FRIEND.

"Once he rigged up an elevator from the top of a barn and nearly broke his neck when the rope snapped. Another time he almost got drowned exploring a fenced-off pothole that was supposed to be bottomless. I guess he was kind of a showoff, but everybody liked him . . . especially the girls."
CLASSMATE HELEN WALTERS.

"Jimmy was different than most boys. He was different in those days because, as I remember, he was often alone. For example, if the baseball team were to practise, often you'd see kids coming together in a car or a pickup, but Jimmy would usually arrive alone . . . I don't recall ever seeing him on dates with girls. I always recall Jimmy riding his motorcycle . . . and I don't ever remember seeing a girl on it."
SCHOOL FRIEND PAUL WEAVER.

"We used to squabble when he was my student. We'd always get back together somehow. Once he offered me a cigarette in class just to be smart. I almost popped him. He was just that kind of maverick kid."
TEACHER ADELINE NALL.

"I never understood him. I never understood what he was after, what sort of person he'd been because he never tried to get on my side of the fence or try to see things the way I saw them when I was little."
DEAN ABOUT HIS FATHER.

"I was always with my mom and we were very close. She used to turn things in the (bath) water for me — she used to put this little boat I had in the water and then she would make the water turn like a whirlpool by turning her finger around and around the boat . . . it used to make me dizzy!

"I'd laugh and laugh and I wanted to do it myself. But what happened was that I would start turning the water around and the boat would flop over upside down and it'd sink. I never understood it — how she could keep it from sinking."

"My mother named me after Lord Byron."

"I grew up in a little Indiana town called Fairmount. I was an only child. My father was a farmer, but he was something of an artist too. He had a remarkable adeptness with his hands."

"Jimmy considered himself an outsider in town, and people in Fairmount quickly regarded him as being different."
WRITER AND CHILDHOOD ACQUAINTANCE JOE HYAMS.

"My town likes industrial impotence
My town's small, loves its diffidence
My town thrives on dangerous bigotry
My town's big in the sense of idolatry
My town believes in God and His crew
My town hates the Catholic and Jew
My town's innocent, selfistic caper
My town's diligent, reads the newspaper
My town's sweet, I was born bare
My town is not what I am, I am here."
POEM BY DEAN WRITTEN INSIDE COPY OF EDWIN HONIG'S
LORCA.

"Having no mother is tough on a kid, you know. But when she died I went to live with my aunt and uncle — great people."

"He shut it all inside him. The only person he could ever have talked about it with was lying there in the casket."
A COUSIN ON DEAN'S RETURN TO INDIANA, AGED NINE, AFTER HIS MOTHER'S DEATH.

"I was never a farmer. I always wanted out of there, but I never ran away because I never wanted to hurt anyone."

"This was a real farm, and I worked like crazy as long as someone was watching me. Forty acres of oats made a huge stage — and when the audience left I took a nap and nothing got ploughed or harrowed. Then I met a friend who lived over in Marion and he taught me how to wrestle and kill cats and other things boys do behind barns. And I began to live."

"I remember one time when I found out that if you give a duck a piece of salt pork, it goes right through him in about ten seconds. So I got me some fishing line and tied a piece of pork to one end and fed it to a big drake. It passed on through and I gave it to another duck and then another, and before long I had the whole barnyard full of ducks all strung together like pearls on a string. You should have heard them quack!"

"The way they had it, you could go to hell just for stepping on a grape."

DEAN'S VERDICT ON AUNT ORTENSE'S TEMPERANCE UNION FRIENDS.

"When I was four or five or six my mother had me playing the violin — I was a goddam child prodigy. My mother also had me tap dancing . . . not at the same time I played the violin, though! She died of cancer when I was eight, and the violin was buried too. I left California — hell, this story *needs* violin music . . ."

"I started the violin when I was a kid, but it didn't take. That was mother's idea. If she hadn't died I'd probably be sawing away yet . . ."

"I was anaemic. I don't know whether I went back to the farm looking for a greater source of life and expression or for blood! Anyway I got healthy . . . and this can be hazardous. You have to assume responsibilities when you're healthy."

"At about 12 or 13, I found out what I was really useful for — to *live*. Why did God put all these things here for us to be interested in?"

"I've been riding since I was 16. I have a motor cycle now. I don't tear around on it but intelligently motivate myself through the quagmire and entanglement of streets."

"I used to ride to school. I used to live with my aunt and uncle. I used to go out for the cows on the motor cycle. Scared the hell out of them. They'd get to running and their udders would start to swing and they'd lose a quart of milk."

"I was that tall . . . and instead of doing little poems about mice I did things like *The Terror Of Death* — the *goriest*! That made me *strange* . . . a little harpy in short pants."

"I had to prove myself and I had the facility to do so. I became very proficient at wielding a paintbrush and sketching."

"I won the state pole vault championship. I was the bright star in basketball. I won the state dramatic declaration contest doing Charles Dickens' *The Madman*. When I got through there were broken bodies lying all over the stage."

"The way I figure it, whatever abilities I have now took shape when I was at high school. I went in for sports like pole vaulting and track events to prove something to myself."

"My father was a farmer, but he did have this remarkable adeptness with his hands. Whatever abilities I may have crystallised there in high school, when I was trying to prove something to myself — that I could do it, I suppose. One of my teachers was a frustrated actress. Through her, I entered and won a state dramatic contest, reciting a Dickens piece called *The Madman*. What's it about? About this real gone cat who knocks off several people. It begins with a scream: I really woke up those judges!

"All these things were good discipline and experience for me. After graduation, I went to live with my father in Los Angeles — mother had died when I was a kid — and just for the hell of it I signed up for a pre-law course at UCLA. That did call for a certain knowledge of histrionics. I even joined a fraternity on the campus, but I busted a couple of guys in the nose and got myself kicked out. I wasn't happy in law, either."

"I became an actor by accident, I guess, though I've always been involved in some kind of theatrical stuff since I was a child — you know, school plays, music and stuff."

"Later on I won a state oratorical contest. I think I might have won the national contest but I didn't go on with it."

"To me, acting is the most logical way for people's neuroses to manifest themselves, in the great need we all have to express ourselves. To my way of thinking, an actor's course is set even before he's out of the cradle."

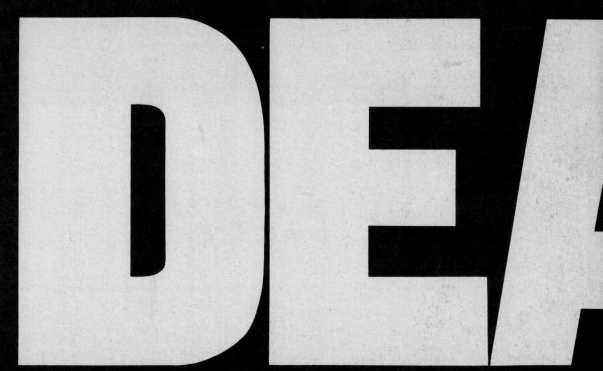

DEA

James Dean In His Own Words

"This very well known actor was acting opposite him, and Jimmy would come up with a different character each time they did the scene. Finally this actor grabbed Jimmy by the tie — no, I mean the shirt front, because Jimmy never wore a tie — and said 'Listen, you son of a bitch, if you give me another interpretation next time I'll wipe the floor with you!'"
MORT ABRAHAMS, TV DIRECTOR.

"It's better to be noticed than ignored."
DEAN TO ADELINE NALL, FAIRMOUNT SCHOOLTEACHER.

"Stories about him being troublesome as an actor are nonsense. He was an enormously imaginative and spontaneous actor. And that, of course, causes disruptions, delays, but it comes from an artistic effort. He was just beginning to get discipline of choice and he was having trouble holding a character once it was set. If I had to make a list of my five most temperamental actors, Jimmy would definitely not be on it."
MORT ABRAHAMS, TV DIRECTOR.

"I seem to be getting a very cheap theatre education. The work I am doing is easy and advancement is unlimited as to talent . . . (but) we get very little pay, if any."
WRITING HOME TO HIS AUNT AND UNCLE ABOUT HIS FIRST THEATRE GROUP.

"The most catty, criticising, narcissistic bunch of people you ever saw, always at each other's throats. But let an outsider try to interfere and they flock together like a bunch of long lost buddies . . . what a life! I learn a lot from them. I've just got to be patient, I guess. They never made it until their twenties, thirties and even forties."
WRITING HOME TO HIS AUNT AND UNCLE ABOUT HIS FIRST THEATRE GROUP.

"God! It's a dream. Don't let anyone wake me up."
ON LEARNING HE'D BEEN CAST IN A UCLA PRODUCTION OF MACBETH, 1950.

"The play was very much of a success . . . I was very much rewarded and proved myself a capable actor in the eyes of several hundred culture-minded individuals. Man, if I can keep this up, and nothing interferes with my progress, one of these days I might be able to contribute something to the world (theatrically)."
LETTER TO AUNT AND UNCLE ABOUT HIS INVOLVEMENT IN A UCLA MACBETH PRODUCTION.

"How do you like being compared to Brando?"
"How do you like being compared to Walter Winchell?"
RIPOSTE TO AN ALSO-RAN NEWSPAPER COLUMNIST.

"Anybody who hasn't seen Harry Bauer doesn't know what movie art can be."

"An actor should always be on the edge of an explosion. Every line he says should be the first and last time he says it. He's got to be sitting on a keg of dynamite. And Jimmy was."
DIRECTOR NICHOLAS RAY, REBEL WITHOUT A CAUSE.

"In motion pictures, you can't fool the camera. If we were doing this on stage, we'd probably be able to gimmick it up — but not in a picture. Film fans are too critical these days."
TO THE LOS ANGELES TIMES ON THE REBEL SET.

"When a new actor comes along, he's always compared to someone else. Brando was compared to Clift, Clift to someone else, Barrymore to Booth and so forth . . . I can only do the best job I can, the realist acting. They can compare me to WC Fields if they want to."
TO ASSOCIATED PRESS REPORTER BOB THOMAS.

"That did it! I didn't have to come in here and listen to this kind of talk. I won't take it, and as far as that job is concerned — you know what you can do with it . . . "
RESPONSE TO DIRECTOR WHO ASKED HIM TO ACT 'LIKE BRANDO WITH A CHIP ON HIS SHOULDER.'

"If you're smoking a cigarette, smoke the cigarette and don't act (it). You have to do something and not show it."
TO GIANT CO-STAR DENNIS HOPPER.

"People were telling me I behaved like Brando before I knew who Brando was. I am neither disturbed by the comparison, nor am I flattered by it. I have my own personal rebellions and don't have to rely on Brando's . . . within myself are expressions just as valid. And I'll have a few years to develop my own — what shall I say? — style."

"I'm a son of a bitch. Here I am in this room, with you. It's fantastic. Like meeting Ibsen or Shaw."
TO SCRIPTWRITER CLIFFORD ODETS.

James Dean In His Own Words

"What a guy. One day when he was in the army, he got tired of it and just got up — walked out — went over the hill. The army never forgave him . . . you've got to admire that kind of nerve."

DEAN ON GRAZIANO'S BOOK *SOMEBODY UP THERE LIKES ME* – HIS NEXT SCHEDULED FILM AT THE TIME OF HIS DEATH.

"How can you measure acting in inches? They're crazy!"

DEAN'S RESPONSE TO CASTING DIRECTORS WHO TOLD HIM HE WAS TOO SHORT TO BE AN ACTOR.

"An artist should be judged on his performance only. All the rest is unimportant."

TO *GIANT* PHOTOGRAPHY DIRECTOR WILLIAM C. MELLOR.

"Don't just hand me this — tell me who I am!"

TO WARNERS EXECUTIVE BILL ORR AT AN (UNSUCCESSFUL) SCREEN TEST FOR THE FILM *BATTLE CRY*.

"It's a lot of money and not much work."

TO NICK ADAMS ON AN OFFER FOR THE PAIR TO GO TO VEGAS AS A STAND-UP COMIC DUO.

"I don't want to be a good actor. I want to be the best actor there is. Told you I'd get to the big town some day."

TO STUDENT FRIEND JIM McCARTHY ON THE EVE OF HIS BROADWAY APPEARANCE IN *THE IMMORALIST*.

"The stage is like a religion: you dedicate yourself to it and suddenly you find that you don't have time to see friends and it's hard for them to understand. You don't see *anybody*."

"Cows, pigs, chickens and horses may not appear to be first rate dramatic coaches, but believe it or not I learned a lot about acting from them. Working on a farm gave me a new insight on life which has been of tremendous help to me in character portrayals."

DEAN IN HIS FIRST WARNER BROTHERS BIOGRAPHY.

"A neurotic person has the necessity to express himself, and my neuroticism expresses itself in the dramatic. Why do most actors act? To express the fantasies in which they have involved themselves."

THE FIRST WARNER BROTHERS BIOGRAPHY.

"Acting is just interpretation. I want to create for myself."

TO SCULPTRESS/SOMETIME TEACHER PEGOT WAREING.

"You are my favourite actor: I'd like to meet you."

TO SIR ALEC GUINNESS.

"A guy could go on knocking his brains out, getting nothing but bit parts for years. There's got to be more."

TO ACTOR/CONFIDANT BILL BAST, THE SAME YEAR AS *HAS ANYBODY SEEN MY GAL?*

"You should read some of the letters I got from old ladies watching television. They tell me about how they want me to wear tighter pants. They have this television club of ladies from 50 to 75 and they sit there checking the cats out, then write these dirty letters. It's really hard to believe."

TO ACTOR/CONFIDANT BILL BAST.

"Nearly all the kids we know are imitating Marlon (Brando). I think he is a truly fine actor but I am not trying to imitate him or anyone else. I am only concerned with finding myself."

TO AN ACTRESS WHILE AT ACTING SCHOOL.

"He'd do something off-beat, like the ashtray crucifixion he created, using two matches placed on top of a heap of sugar he'd poured into the ashtray. When he lit it . . . it would carbonise and make the sugar bubble and crackle into a disgusting black, oozy puddle. Jimmy loved to put on this kind of childish performance."

ACTOR BILLY JAMES.

"To me she's the complete mother image, typifying perfection. Maybe she's the kind of person you'd like to have had for a mother."

DEAN ON GRACE KELLY.

"He's a real hot shoe. When you ride, you wear a steel shoe that goes over the bottom of your boot. When you round a corner, you put that foot out on the ground. When you can *really* ride you're called a hot shoe. Gable rides like crazy."

DEAN ON CLARK GABLE.

"I want to do *Hamlet* soon. Only a young man can play him as he was — with the naïvety. Laurence Olivier played it safe. Something is lost when the older man plays him. They anticipate his answers. You don't feel that Hamlet is thinking — just declaiming. Sonority of voice and technique the old men have. But this kind of Hamlet isn't the stumbling, feeling, reaching, searching boy that he really was."

TO COLUMNIST HEDDA HOPPER.

"Acting is wonderful and immediately satisfying, but my talents lie in directing and beyond that my great fear is writing. That's the god."

"I can't apply the seat of my pants to it right now. I'm too youthful and silly . . . I'm in great awe of writing, and fearful of it. But some day . . . "

"He could not have become a star at any other moment — certainly not if he were shooting today (1961). In 1954 people wanted a boy who was all mixed up . . . Dean is a legend because he is dead. No one like him could now be a star."
ELIA KAZAN.

"By then I had a notion that acting might be the career for me. When I first mentioned acting to dad, he didn't think it was such a hot idea. He'd seen too much Hollywood garbage, and thought I'd be wasting my time."

"Don't get me wrong — I'm not knocking Hollywood. I'm in no position to. After I decided to try my luck in pictures I contacted an agent and got a handful of small parts in movies like *Has Anybody Seen My Gal*? Then there was *Fixed Bayonets*, a Korean War picture. I had one line — it went, 'It's a rear guard coming back.' That was it — what a part!"

"I moved to New York . . . and it turned out to be a wise move. I picked up odd jobs here and there and started at the Actors Studio under Lee Strasberg. Most of what I learned about acting came from that man — he's a walking encyclopedia with a fantastic insight into human behaviour."

"I am frightened by this success — it has all come too early for me. I must try to explain this. I've got a lot of growing up to do, so I've got to be given time to master the art of handling Hollywood — to learn what to say and what not to say."

"What I want to do is to create my own theatre."

"Too many directors and not enough actors."
DEAN'S VERDICT ON UCLA.

"Just forget about the end results. Remember the satisfaction comes in the work and not in the end result. Just remember who you are, and don't take any of their crap out there."
DEAN TO ACTOR/CONFIDANT BILL BAST.

"It teaches me to reach to the back of the theatre and also to overcome my fear of an audience."
EXPLAINING HIS IMITATION OF A SCARECROW DOWN ON THE FARM.

"To be a fine actor you must remember two things: concentration and unlimited imagination. With those, there's no limit to what you can do."
TO YOUNGER ACTOR STEVE ROWLAND.

"An author must interpret life, and in order to do so must be willing to accept all the experiences that life has to offer. In fact he must seek out more of life than life puts at his feet. In the short span of his lifetime, an actor must learn all there is to know, experience all there is to experience, or approach that state as closely as possible. He must be superhuman in his efforts to store away in the core of his subconscious everything that he might be called upon to use in the expression of his art.
  "Nothing should be more important to the artist than life and the living of it, not even the ego. To grasp the full significance of life is the actor's duty, to interpret it his problem, and to explain it his dedication . . . Being an actor is the loneliest thing in the world. You are all alone with your concentration and your imagination, and that is all you have. Being a good actor isn't easy. Being a man is even harder. I want to be both before I'm done."

"I always think that my best is yet to come. And when it does arrive, I know that I shall not be satisfied."

"To me, acting is the most logical way for a man with problems to express himself. I think all of us have a great need to let go. Acting is my outlet."

James Dean In His Own Words

"An actor should know a little about many things. He must do more than just project his personality on the screen. He should represent a cross section of many phases of life. The best way to succeed in this is to learn as much as possible about people and their pursuits. Any person stagnates if he does not add to his knowledge. I know that I feel more alive when I'm trying to master something new."

"Those chairs they make you wait on are made scientifically so that in exactly 11 minutes your backside begins to hurt. But I beat the average. First I sit on one half of my fanny, then on the other. They don't get rid of me until my 22 minutes are up. But I'm beginning to take the shape of those chairs. Maybe that's the shape of my destiny."
DOING THE ROUNDS OF NEW YORK CITY AGENTS.

"The character does many things that the character shouldn't do — and you have to select the reading from your mind where your faults are, where your problems are, where you constantly fall back on the security that made you so successful . . . To go ahead and develop and to attempt and to try. For instance today my emotional apparatus won't do it, I don't know, plugged up or something. It's not kinda easy for me."
EXPLAINING THE RELATIONSHIP BETWEEN THE SCRIPT AND THE FINISHED FILM.

"I practised for years in the middle of a wheat field in Indiana."
REVEALING WHERE HE LEARNED *HAMLET*.

"Dean was filled with the Method. If one of his characters was sick he would actually want to vomit on camera."
FRIEND MARTY LANDAU.

"I was nervous. I'm a Method actor, I work through my senses. If you're nervous, your senses can't reach your subconscious and that's that — you can't work. So I figured if I could piss in front of those two thousand people, man, and I could be cool, I figured if I could do that, I could get in front of the camera and do just anything, anything at all."
AFTER URINATING IN PUBLIC ON THE *GIANT* SET.

"Every part of you's got to be in there pitching — every inch of you, every second. When Brando was doing Stanley Kowalski (in *A Streetcar Named Desire*), he didn't let down *once*. Man, he was *great* . . ."

"I had a motorbike before *he* did!"
TO PHOTOGRAPHER ROY SCHATT ON BRANDO.

"I don't want to be just a good actor. I don't even want to be just the best. I want to grow and grow so tall *nobody* can reach me. Not to prove anything, but just to go where you ought to go when you devote your whole life and all you are to one thing."

"I owe such a lot to him: he saved me when I got all mixed up. One thing he said helped me more than anything. He told me that I didn't know the difference between acting as a soft job and acting as a difficult art. He told me it didn't take much to be just another ham, but that to make a part stand out — to make it live for the audience — that was another thing altogether.
    "Then he asked me why I wanted to be an actor — for the money and the applause, or for the art? Darned if I knew! I'd never thought about that . . . not that way. So then he said I had better find out or I'd never amount to anything. I said 'Where do I find out?' And he said 'Not hanging around Hollywood. Go to New York and learn something about the stage.' So I did."
ACKNOWLEDGING THE INFLUENCE OF TUTOR JAMES WHITMORE.

"You won't believe how I used to walk around and try to see these people. I mean, the ones that have the positions — the ones that were doing the casting and I knew there were parts being cast that I was perfect for . . ."
IN HOLLYWOOD AS A NOBODY.

"This guy in Hollywood — he's a friend of mine. He's a cameraman and showed me a lot of things. And now I want to make a movie. I'd like to try, I've learned a lot. I watched him. It's no big deal. You put what you want in a frame. It's a cinch."
ON FUTURE FILM-MAKING AMBITIONS.

"It was really going on around me all the time, and I'd stop somewhere like in the windows of that Coffee Dan's on Vine Street because that was across the road from NBC and I was always trying to get something over there. If it was a little part I didn't care what it was, but there were times when I looked at myself in the window and I looked weird, man, weird. It was like I wasn't real any more, and I was this kind of kid going around but Hollywood was coming up over me . . ."

"Once when my car wasn't running I had blood in my shoes because I had blisters from walking around all over there — no matter how much I'd go around and see these people it wasn't going to happen for me and I got lost. Simple as that — I got lost."

"I remember the first time I had to get the make-up on. I sat there and the make-up guy said 'Rest your head back and keep your chin up' and he slapped it on. I knew then, squinting at the mirror, where and what I was supposed to be."

"Success is only in the mechanics of it. All the rest I have because I'm me and I've got it all."
TO ACTOR PAT HENCHIE.

"Fatima (fate) . . . I gotta be faithful to her. It's predestined that I'm going to make it and that I'm going to make it like Marlon (Brando) and that I'm going to be a gigantic movie star."

"See, this is exactly what movies are all about. That scene is the epitome . . ."
ON A SCENE IN *FROM HERE TO ETERNITY* WHEN MONTGOMERY CLIFT TELLS DONNA REED HE CAN'T BOX BECAUSE HE ONCE BLINDED SOMEONE.

"I know I have done wrong by not taking care of the ticket before now, but I was afraid. Yes, sir. You see, I'm a student at UCLA and I've been having a right time of it, I mean with money. I don't have much and what I do have goes mostly on food and books. I know 25 dollars doesn't sound much to you your honour, but to me it could mean food for a whole month or books for a whole semester.
    "I never would have done it your honour if I hadn't promised my father that I'd have the car back that afternoon at five. He let me borrow it so I could go to an interview for a part, the job I needed. I guess I just didn't want to let my father down . . ."
HIS BEST EVER OFF-STAGE PERFORMANCE IN A VAN NUYS COURTROOM AFTER FAILING TO SETTLE A 25 DOLLAR SPEEDING TICKET. THE JUDGE LET HIM OFF WITH A FIVE DOLLAR FINE.

"You're every bit as good as you think you are. But it's going to be a long time and hard work making other people understand that."
AGENT JANE DEACY.

"Jimmy was as blind as a bat without his glasses, but he wouldn't wear them when he was acting. In one scene he was supposed to be in the middle of the stage, and I was supposed to come in and trip over him. He couldn't find the middle and went all the way to the end. If I'd tripped over him I'd have been off-stage."
CHRISTINE WHITE, ACTRESS.

"I have made great strides in my craft. After months of auditioning I am very proud to announce that I am a member of the Actors Studio. The greatest school of the theatre. It houses great people, like Marlon Brando, Julie Harris, Arthur Kennedy, Elia Kazan, Mildred Dunnock, Kevin McCarthy, Monty Clift, June Havoc and on and on and on. Very few get into it, and it is absolutely free. It is the best thing that can happen to an actor. I am one of the youngest to belong."
LETTER TO UNCLE AND AUNT ON JOINING THE ACTORS STUDIO.

"Everyone got the idea that it was a sloppily dressed, don't-give-a-damn kind of group. That is not so. To begin with, Dean was scarcely at the studio at all. He came in a few times and slouched in the front row, he never participated in anything."
LEE STRASBERG, DIRECTOR, ACTORS STUDIO.

"I don't know what's inside of me. I don't know what happens when I act . . . but if I let them dissect me like a rabbit in a clinical research laboratory or something then I might not be able to produce again. They might sterilise me. That man (director Lee Strasberg) had no right to tear me down like that. You keep knocking a guy down and you take the guts away from him. And what's an actor without guts?"
TO ACTOR/CONFIDANT BILL BAST.

"You know, I think the greatest actors in the world are Paul Muni, Laurence Olivier and Marlon Brando."

"Jimmy used to call Montgomery Clift when he was in New York and say, 'I'm a great actor and you're my idol, and I need to see you because I need to talk to you and I need to communicate.' And Clift would change his phone number. Then after Jimmy was dead Monty Clift saw all three of his films and every time he'd get drunk and cry about the fact he'd denied this young man the opportunity of seeing him and talking to him."
ACTOR DENNIS HOPPER.

WARNER BROS. STU
WARDROBE TEST
FOR
#403 GIANT
OF
JAMES DEAN
AS
JETT

WARDROBE CHANGE # 8

WORN IN (SET EXT HIGHWA
(SCENE 277A

 55

"As of now (1955), I don't see myself as specifically belonging to either. The cinema is a very truthful medium because the camera doesn't let you get away with anything. On-stage, you can even loaf a little, if you're so inclined. Technique, on the other hand, is more important. My real aim, my real goal, is to achieve what I call camera-functioning on the stage. Not that I'm down on Hollywood . . .

"Don't get me wrong I'm not one of the wise ones who try to put Hollywood down. It just so happens that I fit to cadence and pace better here (New York) as far as living goes. New York is vital, above all fertile. They're a little harder to find, maybe, but out there in Hollywood, behind all that brick and mortar, there are human beings just as sensitive to fertility. The problem for this cat — myself — is not to get lost."

"When an actor plays a scene exactly the way a director orders, it isn't acting. It's following instructions. Anyone with the physical qualifications can do that. So the director's task is just that — to direct, to point the way. Then the actor takes over. And he must be allowed the space, the freedom to express himself in the role. Without that space, an actor is no more than an unthinking robot with a chestful of push buttons."

"When you know there is something more to go in a character, and you're not sure what it is, you just got to go out after it. Walk out on the tight rope. If the rope's hard it's got to be leading somewhere."
TO FELLOW ACTOR DENNIS HOPPER.

"Look, this bit I'm doing is a wild one. It's a Dickens thing called *The Madman* and I've got to go crazy in it. How the heck can I go crazy in a shirt and tie? It wouldn't work. I can't do the piece if I don't feel it, and I can't feel it all duded up."
TO FELLOW STUDENT JIM McCARTHY BEFORE DEBATING COMPETITION.

"Performers are always being looked at. I wonder what it feels like to be inside and look out. Stay outside and photograph people's reactions to me just sitting there staring out . . ."
POSING AS A SHOP WINDOW DUMMY FOR DENNIS STOCK IN NEW YORK'S SIXTH AVENUE.

"I have registered for summer and fall sessions at UCLA. I take an English exam Monday. I am now a fully fledged member of the *Miller Playhouse Theatre Guild* troop. I wasn't in time to be cast in any production, but my knowledge of the stage and the ability to design and paint sets won me the place of head stage manager for the next production of four one-act plays starting Thursday."
LETTER TO HIS GRANDPARENTS.

"The biggest thrill of my life came three weeks ago, after a week of gruelling auditions for UCLA's four major theatrical productions, the major one being *Macbeth* which will be presented in Royce Hall (seats 160). After the auditioning of 1600 actors and actresses, I came up with a wonderful lead in *Macbeth*, the character being Malcolm (huge part) . . ."
LETTER TO AUNT AND COUSIN, 1950.

"Hey, you know, man, I'm doing this cowboy for TV and this guy's gotta pull his gun. Got to pull his gun fast, you know. So I got to have quick fingers."
EXPLAINING WHY HE BIT THE TIPS OF HIS FINGERS TO KEEP THEM SENSITIVE.

"Because I hate my mother and father. I wanted to get up on stage . . . and I wanted to show them. I'll tell you what made me want to become an actor, what gave me that drive to want to be the best. My mother died when I was nine. I used to sneak out of my uncle's house at night and go to her grave and I used to cry on her grave — 'Mother, why did you leave me? Why did you leave me? I need you . . .'"
EXPLAINING HIS EARLIEST MOTIVATION TO ACT TO DENNIS HOPPER.

"I don't want to burn myself out . . . I've made three pictures in the last two years."
TO REPORTER AFTER *GIANT*.

James Dean In His Own Words

Hollywood

"You know, it gets sickening. The other day we were sitting at the pool and I made a bet with Rogers that the names of La Rue or the Mocambo would be dropped at least 15 times within the next hour. We kept count and I won. What a pile of . . ."
TO ACTOR/CONFIDANT BILL BAST.

"They'll never give me a real chance out here. I'm not the bobby-sox type, and I'm not the romantic leading-man type either. Can you imagine me making love to Lana Turner?"
TO STRUGGLING FELLOW ACTOR IN HOLLYWOOD.

"I can't stomach this dung home any more."
TO ACTOR/CONFIDANT BILL BAST ON LEAVING HOLLYWOOD FOR NEW YORK.

"I don't like it here. I don't like people here . . . I want to die. I have told the girls here to kiss my ass and what sterile stupid prostitutes they were . . . haven't seen the sun yet (fog and smog) . . . I look like a prune."
LETTER TO ACTRESS BARBARA GLENN IN NEW YORK FROM HOLLYWOOD.

"I came to Hollywood to act, not to charm society . . . the objective artist has always been misunderstood. I probably should have a press agent. But I don't care what people write about me. I'll talk to (reporters) I like; the others can print whatever they please."
TO *ASSOCIATED PRESS* REPORTER BOB THOMAS.

"What a pile of hogwash. They've got in their heads they're gods. This town is full of them. They get these poor lads — saps like me — and make them perform. You know, run around like lost goats and charming the pants off important people. I thought it might pay off. But it doesn't take long to find out it won't. And if I can't make it on my talent I don't want to make it at all."
TO ACTOR/CONFIDANT BILL BAST.

"You come in here braying like an ass when we're in the middle of a conference. Haven't you got any manners? (Aside) That loudmouthed slob. Four years ago he gave me a hard time on an interview here."
SETTLING OLD SCORES IN HIS WEST COAST AGENT'S OFFICES.

New York

"Three ball parks. Three ball parks in one town. Gee, I'm coming to Manhattan some time. I don't know when, but I'm coming.
TO FELLOW SCHOLAR (AND NEW YORK RESIDENT) JIM McCARTHY, 1949.

"I've discovered a whole new world here, a whole new way of thinking . . . this town's the end. It's talent that counts here. You've got to stay with it or get lost. I like it."
TO ACTOR/CONFIDANT BILL BAST ON NEW YORK.

"I got a kick out of the whole thing. Fifth Avenue, the dogs, the walk, and goddam it, this diner and the way it looks. It's a swell place to live."
EXPLAINING TO PHOTOGRAPHER ROY SCHATT WHY HE LIKED NEW YORK.

"This place reminds me of a Hollywood breakaway set. They'd roll away that half with the coffee urns and the camera would get here to shoot us and get the booths, the windows and the outside. When they wanted to shoot the counter, this side would roll away for the camera and crew."
COMPARING A TWELFTH AVENUE NEW YORK CAFÉ (THE REAL THING) TO A FAKE HOLLYWOOD SET.

"In the pensiveness of night the cheap, monotonous, shrill, symbolic, sensual beat of suggestive drums tattoos orgyistic images on my brain. The smell of gin and 90 per cent beer entwine with the sometimes suspenseful slow, sometimes laboured static, sometimes motionless, sometimes painfully rigid, till finally the long awaited for jerks and convulsions that fill the now thick chewing gum haze with a mist of sweat, fling the patrons into a fit of suppressed joy."
DESCRIBING NEW YORK'S CLUBLAND TO ACTRESS/SOMETIME GIRLFRIEND BARBARA GLENN.

"I, James Byron Dean, was born on February 8, 1931, in Marion, Indiana. My parents, Winton Dean and Mildred Dean, formerly Mildred Wilson, existed in the state of Indiana until I was six years of age.

"Dad's work with the Government caused a change, so dad as a dental mechanic was transferred to California. There we lived until the fourth year. Mom became ill and passed out of my life at the age of nine. I never knew the reason for mom's death, in fact it still preys on my mind.

"I had always lived such a talented life. I studied violin, played in concerts, tap-danced on theatre stages but most of all I like art, to mould and create things with my hands.

"I came back to Indiana to live with my Uncle. I lost the dancing and violin, but not the art. I think my life will be devoted to art and dramatics. And there are so many different fields of art it would be hard to foul up. And if I did there are so many different things to do — farm, sports, science, geology, coaching, teaching, music. I got it, and I know that if I better myself there will be no match. A fellow must have confidence.

"When living in California, my young eyes experienced many things. It was also my luck to make three visiting trips to Indiana, going and coming a different route each time. I have been in almost every state west of Indiana. I remember all.

"My hobby, or what I do in my spare time, is motorcycling. I know a lot about them mechanically and I love to ride. I have been in for races and done well. I own a small cycle myself. When I'm not doing this, I'm usually engaged in athletics, the heartbeat of any American boy. As one tries to make a goal in a game, there should be a goal in this crazy world for each of us. I hope I know where mine is anyway, I'm after it.

"I don't mind telling you Mr Dubois, this is the hardest subject to write about considering the information one knows of oneself."

DEAN'S FIRST RECORDED HIGH SCHOOL ESSAY.

"Never had much and don't need much. If the Army wants me, I'm ready."

ON FACING THE DRAFT.

"What counts to the artist is performance, not publicity. Guys who don't know me, already they've typed me as an oddball."

"What the hell good are socks without shoes?"

ARRIVING AT A TV COMMERCIAL BAREFOOT AFTER SHRINKING HIS SHOES ON A RADIATOR.

"I can't get away because I'm playing this game . . . and it's on my own terms. I'm going to play it through for a while until I get all that's necessary out of it. That part won't matter because they aren't going to catch me."

"I wouldn't like me if I had to be around me."

"Maybe publicity is important but I just can't make it, can't get on with it. I've been told by a lot of guys the way it works. The newspapers give you a big build-up, something happens, they tear you down. Who needs it? Maybe I'm naïve when I resent the prying into my off-camera life, but for the life of me I can't see how a communicative power based on the Mocambo, and a stack of press clippings helps an actor to turn in a better performance. Nobody is going to buy tickets to see me just because I give a fine interview — or because I let some stooge ask how it feels to be the second Marlon Brando."

"Geographical location means nothing to me. A man can produce no matter where the hell he is."

"We'll hitch hike out there . . . it's only 800 miles."

INVITING HIS FRIENDS TO INDIANA . . . FOR THE WEEKEND.

"I think the prime reason for existence, for living in this world, is discovery."

"No one ever did anything for me. I don't owe anything to anyone."

TO THE PRESS AFTER *EAST OF EDEN*.

"It makes me look like a kid . . . a helpless kid who just got his finger banged or his best toy busted and he wants his mother. It makes me look like I'm hurt and I'm crying out — not out loud — but just crying for someone to come and help me. I don't want people to see me that way. Maybe later, much later, you can print the picture — but not for a long, long time."

TO PHOTOGRAPHER FRANK WORTH, REJECTING A PHOTOGRAPH.

"We killed 34 rabbits last night: that makes 104 to date. If we hadn't gotten the coyote, it would have killed that lamb. Sure as shooting it would have killed that lamb.

"I'm not going to kill rabbits or birds or anything any more. They don't do anybody any harm."

HUNTING DURING *GIANT* WITH DIALOGUE COACH BOB HINKLE.

"People sit and listen to me until they say something that fits in with what they figure I'd be like. That's the part they write down. Then they say, 'Dean, ughh! That character'."

TO *SEVENTEEN* MAGAZINE.

"The last time I was in this store, nobody paid any attention to me. I was too small. All of a sudden, I guess I've grown a few inches."

ON SHOPPING TRIP, FACED WITH A FAWNING ASSISTANT.

"I'm a small town boy, born in a small town with small town ideas. That's how I want to live. I intend some day to retire and farm."

"I'm a serious minded, intense little devil, terribly gauche and so tense I don't see how people stay in the same room as me. I know I wouldn't tolerate myself."

TO PHILLIP K. SCHEUER, *LOS ANGELES TIMES*.

"In a certain sense I am (fatalistic). I don't exactly know how to explain it, but I have a hunch there are some things in life that we just can't avoid. They'll happen to us probably because we're built that way — we simply attract our own fate . . . make our own destiny.

"I think I'm like the Aztecs in that respect, too. With their sense of doom, they tried to get the most out of life while life was good. And I go along with them on that philosophy. I don't mean the 'eat, drink and be merry for tomorrow we die' idea, but something a lot deeper and more valuable. I want to live as intensely as I can. Be as useful and helpful to others as possible, for one thing. But live for myself as well. I want to feel things and experiences right down to their roots . . . enjoy the good in life while it is good."

TO NEW YORK RADIO HOST JACK SHAFER.

"I've always been fascinated by the Aztec Indians. They were a very fatalistic people . . . and I sometimes share that feeling. They had such a weird sense of doom that when the warlike Spaniards arrived in Mexico lots of the Aztecs just gave up fatalistically to an event they believed couldn't be avoided."

TO JACK SHAFER.

"I hate anything that limits progress and growth. I hate institutions that do this; a way of acting . . . a way of thinking. I hope this doesn't make me sound like a Communist. Communism is the most limiting factor of all today."

ONE OF DEAN'S RARE POLITICAL STATEMENTS.

"I dig Gandhi the most."

ANOTHER OF DEAN'S RARE POLITICAL STATEMENTS.

"My purpose in life does not include a hankering to charm society."

"Every person has to find his real self. The maxim 'Know Thyself' is worth trying to follow. Like a lot of other people, I'm searching in the only way I know how."

"The trouble with me is that I'm just dog tired. Everybody hates me and thinks I'm a heel. They say I've gone Hollywood, but honestly I'm just the same as when I didn't have a dime. I'm tired. I went into *Giant* immediately after a long hard schedule in *Rebel*. Maybe I'd just better go away."

"Stop it, don't do it with him. It's me you should be making love to. I'm the star, I'm the important one. I've been in a movie and a play. It's me you should be kissing."

TO A FELLOW ACTOR'S NEW GIRLFRIEND.

James Dean In His Own Words

"It's a surrealist joke, like Dali's soft watches that can't work, yet tell the goddamned time, man. It's dear old Dali. Dali with a fringe on top."
EXPLAINING WHY HE WAS PHOTOGRAPHING TOURISTS IN NEW YORK WITH NO FILM IN HIS CAMERA.

"Don't you think I look like Michelangelo's David?"
TO PHOTOGRAPHER ROY SCHATT AS HE TOOK THE FAMOUS 'TORN SWEATER' SERIES OF PICTURES.

"Don't you sons of bitches ever get bored? I just wanted to spark things, man, that's all. Look at you. Before I did it, we were all sitting quietly eating and drinking, and outside a lot of nine-to-fivers were going home to their wives, like they do every night. Now you're all juiced up, and so are they, man. They'll talk about it for years . . ."
AFTER STOPPING THE MANHATTAN TRAFFIC BY SITTING, SMOKING, IN THE MIDDLE OF THE ROAD IN A CHAIR.

"Old Hemingway squeezed the juice out of life . . . I'm not going to live past 30."
TO PHOTOGRAPHER ROY SCHATT.

"Hemingway is the perfect hero! You can't name anyone as rugged."

"Some day when I make it, I'm determined that they sell this place and move to a healthier, better climate where mom's arthritis won't bother her so much. I'll see to it that they have the life they deserve without all the work and worry . . ."
DEAN'S ASPIRATIONS FOR AUNT ORTENSE AND UNCLE MARCUS.

"Why the hell must I change? No bastard's telling me what to do."

"Everything I've done has been on my own terms. I'll take orders from no one."

"I don't want to stay at the Algonquin (Hotel) anyway. Only Indians stay there . . . when I walked up to the desk the man asked me if I had a reservation."
TO ACTOR/CONFIDANT BILL BAST.

"I've just no faith in this guy. I'm being conned by this bum who's just taking my dough."
TO AGENT JANE DEACY ON HIS ANALYST.

"Have you ever had the feeling that it's not in your hands? I mean, do you ever just know you've got something to do and you've got no control over it? And the truth is I've got to do something. I don't know exactly what it is yet. But when the time comes I'll know. I've got to keep trying until I hit the right thing. See what I mean?"
TO ACTOR/CONFIDANT BILL BAST.

"If you're not afraid, if you take everything you are, everything worthwhile in you, and direct it at one goal, one ultimate mark, you've got to get there. If you start accepting the world, let things happen to you, *around* you, things will happen like you never dreamed they'd happen."

"I was cramming like fellows used to do for exams at school, only my exam was life itself."
STUDYING PIANO AND DANCE.

"When they talk about success they talk about reaching the top. Well, there is no top. You've got to go on and on, not stop at any point."

"I want to grow away from all this crap. You know the petty little world we exist in. I want to leave it all behind, all the petty little thoughts about the unimportant little things that'll be forgotten 100 years from now anyway. There's a level; somewhere where everything is solid and important. I'm going to try to reach up there and find a place I know is pretty close to perfect, a place where this whole messy world should be, could be, if it would just take the time to learn."

"Don't ever put my fucking picture up in here. What do you think, that I live here or something? You think you own me. Nobody owns me."
ON RIPPING DOWN A PICTURE OF HIM IN THE STUDIO CANTEEN.

James Dean In His Own Words

"You're running so fast it's all passing you by . . . You've got to give and receive, you've got to bounce the ball."

TO ACTOR/CONFIDANT BILL BAST.

"We are all impaled on the crock of conditioning. A fish that is in the water has no choice that he is. Genius would have it that we swim in sand. We are fish and we drown. We remain in our world and wonder. The fortunate are taught to ask why. No one can answer."

LETTER TO FAIRMOUNT MENTOR REVEREND DEWEERD.

"If you're gonna throw that pudding away, can I have it? . . . Man, anything would taste good right now. I haven't had anything to eat in two days."

TO TV WRITER FRANK WAYNE WHILE STARVING IN NEW YORK BETWEEN JOBS.

"Sight is bent to lick your heart
A liquid mouth dilutes my thought
Souls knit a nebulae mat
We live here in every world
Secret loft in azure habitat."

INSCRIBED BY DEAN ON THE FLYLEAF OF A PAPERBACK BOOK.

"I'm really kind and gentle. Things get mixed up all the time. I see a person I would like to be very close to (everybody) then I think it would be just the same as before and they don't give a shit for me. Then I say something nasty or nothing at all and walk away. The poor person doesn't know what's happened. He doesn't realise that I have decided I don't like him. What's wrong with people?"

LETTER TO ACTRESS/SOMETIME GIRLFRIEND BARBARA GLENN FROM HOLLYWOOD.

"Hey — I'm a Picasso!"

POSING FOR PHOTOGRAPHER ROY SCHATT WITH GLASSES TO THE SIDE OF THE HEAD, A 'THREE-EYED' EFFECT.

"Got my annual thrill yacht racing for the New York Yacht Club. We had a storm, had to lock ourselves to the helm. I'm a great sailor you know. I got seasick, wasn't worth a god damn."

RECOUNTING A WEEKEND AT SEA TO ACTRESS/SOMETIME GIRLFRIEND BARBARA GLENN.

"Look at it as protective coloration. If I conform to myself, the only one I'm hurting with the press is myself. So instead, I'm a nice, polite, well-raised young boy, full of respect — which is what Hedda likes. Instead of being on my back, she'll be on my side and and defend me against the other press, the people who say I'm just an irrepressible, no-good rebel."

TO HOLLYWOOD WRITER JOE HYAMS ON HIS RELATIONSHIP WITH COLUMNIST HEDDA HOPPER.

"Change is the nature of genius."

TO FAIRMOUNT MENTOR REVEREND DEWEERD FROM NEW YORK.

"I collect everything from twelfth and thirteenth century music to the extreme moderns — you know, Schönberg, Berg, Stravinsky. I also like Sinatra's 'Songs For Young Lovers' album."

"Whatever's inside making me what I am, it's like film. Film only works in the dark. Tear it all open and let in the light and you kill it."

TO GIANT CO-STAR NICK ADAMS.

"It's a toss-off: they say for me to love my father. I could have told them that 15 years ago."

TALKING WITH ADAMS ABOUT HIS ANALYST.

"I saw this knife, and I've been wanting one . . . I just had to have it. But I figured I couldn't betray you entirely so I memorised the script for the reading."

EXPLAINING TO SEE THE JAGUAR AUTHOR N. RICHARD NASH WHY HE'D SPENT THE MONEY GIVEN TO HIM FOR NEW GLASSES ON A KNIFE.

"You think you need understanding? Who do you think you are? I could use a little myself! . . . you're probably running around up there with all those handsome guys. When I get my boat, you'll be sorry. Hope you're OK. Working pretty hard, I guess. More than can be said for us poor thespians back here in the city. Got to move out of this crappy old apartment. Can't get along with nobody, I guess. Makes you feel good when you're not wanted."

LETTER TO ACTRESS/SOMETIME GIRLFRIEND BARBARA GLENN.

"Some men bet on horses or dogs. I gamble on myself."

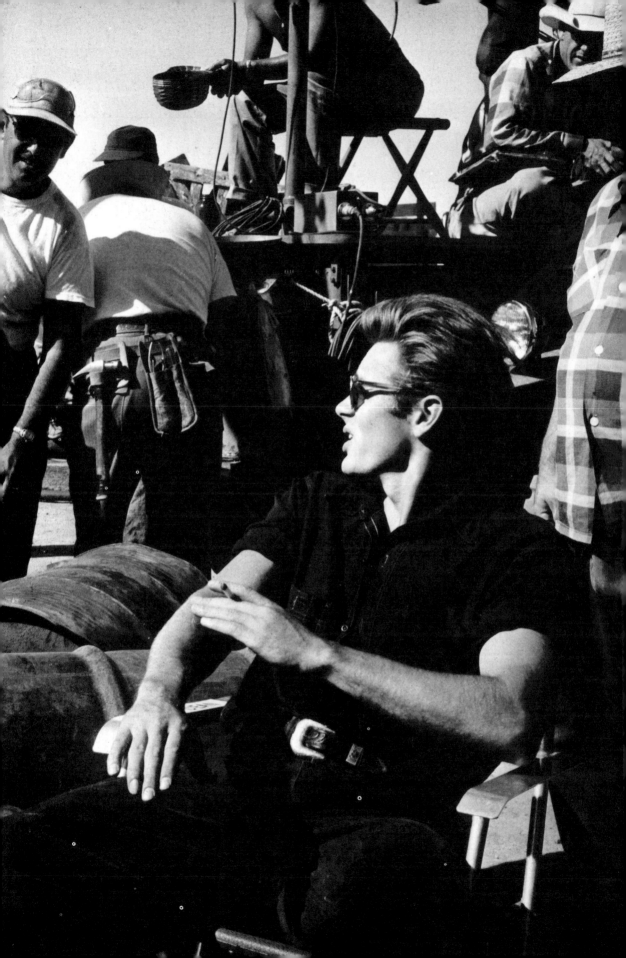

DEA

James Dean In His Own Words

Early Appearances

"It's a rear guard coming back."
DEAN'S ONE LINE IN HIS FIRST SPEAKING PART, *FIXED BAYONETS*, 1951. IT ENDED UP ON THE CUTTING ROOM FLOOR.

"That guy's a professional . . ."
DEAN'S FIRST (SCREENED) WORDS IN THE CINEMA, IN *SAILOR BEWARE*.

"I build up this head of steam like in Jimmy Whitmore's exercises — but where in class you then let it rip, on film you've got to keep it all bottled up. It makes me look like my bladder's bursting!"
TO ACTOR NICK ADAMS ON THE SET OF *HILL NUMBER ONE*, HIS FIRST FILM APPEARANCE, 1951.

"Mr Shumlin, why are you insulting my intelligence?"
WHEN TOLD IN REHEARSAL HOW TO READ HIS FIRST LINE ON *THE IMMORTALIST* BY DIRECTOR HERMAN SHUMLIN. SHUMLIN WAS FIRED, DEAN STAYED.

"Hey, Gramps, I'll have a choc malt, heavy on the choc, plenty of milk, four spoons of malt, two scoops of vanilla ice cream, one mixed and one floating . . ."
TO CHARLES COBURN IN *HAS ANYBODY SEEN MY GAL?*, 1952.

"Only an ice cream freak could get that load of garbage right first time."
DEAN'S REACTION AFTER FLUFFING THREE CONSECUTIVE TAKES.

"I was stunned by the realisation that, no time during the performance, had I been aware that I was watching my friend James Dean. He had so completely created an illusion for me and the rest of the audience that I had believed in Wally Wilkins, the part he was playing — not Jimmy Dean, the boy I knew."
ACTOR/CONFIDANT BILL BAST ON DEAN'S BROADWAY DÉBUT IN *SEE THE JAGUAR*, DECEMBER 1952.

"James Dean adds an extraordinary performance in an almost impossible role, that of a bewildered lad who has been completely shut off from the world by an overzealous mother and who is coming upon both the beauty and brutality of the mountain for the first time."
WALTER KERR, *NEW YORK TRIBUNE*. THE PLAY CLOSED AFTER SIX PERFORMANCES.

"Rehearsals are quite confusing at this point. Lighting etc. Can't tell much about the show yet. Looks like a piece of shit to me. Stereophonic staging and 3-D actors. Probably be a monster success . . . hate this fucking brown make-up."
FIRST IMPRESSIONS OF *THE IMMORALIST* TO ACTRESS/ SOMETIME GIRLFRIEND BARBARA GLENN.

"I am now a colourful, thieving, blackmailing Arab boy played by James Dean. Don't know who the hell I am. They are rewriting a lot. In rehearsals I was working for the elements of tragedy. A real tragedian's role, pathos, etc. I turn out to be the comic relief. The Leon Errol of the show. Balls."
LATER IMPRESSION OF *THE IMMORALIST*.

East Of Eden

"You're going to meet a boy, and he's going to be very strange to you, and he's going to be different. No matter what you see or what you think of him, when you see him on the screen he's gonna be pure gold."
DIRECTOR OF *EAST OF EDEN* ELIA KAZAN TO THE CAST ON INTRODUCING DEAN.

"I cast Jimmy because he was Cal. There was no point in attempting to cast it better. Jimmy was it. He had a grudge against all fathers. He was vengeful, he had a sense of aloofness and of being persecuted; and he was suspicious."
DIRECTOR ELIA KAZAN.

"Have been dejected and extremely moody last two weeks. Have been telling everyone to fuck off, and that's no good I couldn't make them believe I was working on my part. Poor Julie Harris doesn't know what to do with me. Well to hell with her, she doesn't have to do anything to me."
LETTER TO ACTRESS/SOMETIME GIRLFRIEND BARBARA GLENN DURING REHEARSALS.

"Gadge Kazan and Williams are nice, but I wouldn't trust the sons a bitches as far's I can throw 'em. They can take advantage of you like anyone else."
LETTER TO ACTRESS/SOMETIME GIRLFRIEND BARBARA GLENN.

"All of us felt we were right there with him. Many of the movements of Cal Trask were characteristic movements of James Dean. His funny little laugh which ripples with the slightest provocation, his quick jerky springy walks and actions, his sudden change from frivolity to gloom — all were like Jim used to do."
FORMER TEACHER ADELINE NALL ON *EAST OF EDEN*.

"We spent all afternoon and he couldn't do (a scene) right. So I got him loaded on red wine that night. He couldn't drink a lot because he was sort of unstable and liquor would affect him, but I gave him two drinks of wine and he did the scene great."
DIRECTOR ELIA KAZAN.

"I can't divert into being a social human being when I'm working on a hero like Cal, who's essentially demonic."
TO COLUMNIST LOUELLA PARSONS.

"*East Of Eden* is a study in dualities — that it is necessary to arrive at goodness through a sense of the Satanic rather than the puritanic . . . I considered it a great challenge to reveal honestly the things in my part that were of myself as well as the character."

"He really wanted to look uptight. So to get himself really uncomfortable, he told me he didn't pee all day until they did the shot."
DENNIS HOPPER ON DEAN'S *EAST OF EDEN* PERFORMANCE.

"Why should I go? I know I was good, and having people tell me so would only embarrass me."
EXPLAINING HIS ABSENCE AT THE *EAST OF EDEN* PREMIÈRE TO ACTRESS CHRISTINE WHITE.

"Dean's body was very graphic: it was almost writhing in pain sometimes. He was very twisted almost like a cripple or a spastic of some kind. He couldn't do anything straight. He even walked like a crab, as if he were cringing all the time."
DIRECTOR ELIA KAZAN.

"I just want to make this picture and get back to New York. I don't need Hollywood . . . maybe they don't need me either, but I've got the advantage. I've got something they want and they're going to have to pay to get it."
DEAN DURING *EAST OF EDEN*.

"I wanted that part in *Eden* so bad I could taste it. Every time I went to read for a part in New York this clown would be there."
ACTOR PAUL NEWMAN ON DEAN.

"We began to suspect something outstanding was going to happen with him about three-quarters of the way through the picture. You could see that he was just so good. I've never seen anything like it in the movies in my whole life including Marlon Brando."
DIRECTOR ELIA KAZAN.

"I played an Arab in *The Immoralist* on Broadway and got an award for it. Then came the *East Of Eden* film under the direction of Elia Kazan.
"No, I didn't read the novel. The way I work I'd much rather justify myself with the adaptation rather than the source. I felt I wouldn't have any trouble — too much, anyway — with this characterisation once we started because I think I understood the part. I knew, too, that if I had any problems over the boy's background I could straighten it out with Kazan."
DEAN EXPLAINS *EAST OF EDEN* TO THE *NEW YORK TIMES'* HOWARD THOMPSON.

"I remember the last day of filming . . . I went up to the caravan and knocked on the door and I thought I heard something like a sob. I said 'Jimmy', and then knocked again. So then I was sure it was a sob, and I opened the door and he was just in tears, and I said what's the matter and he said 'It's over, it's over' and he was like a little boy. So lovely . . ."
EAST OF EDEN CO-STAR JULIE HARRIS.

Rebel Without A Cause

"The thing that interested me in *Rebel* was doing something that would counteract *The Wild One*. I went out and hung around with kids in Los Angeles before making the movie. Some of them even called themselves 'Wild Ones'. They wear leather jackets, go out looking for someone to rough up a little. These aren't poor kids, you know. Lots of them have money, grow up and become pillars of the community. Boy, they scared me! But it's a constructive movie, it gives some of these kids — the ones who aren't out to be tough guys — something to identify with."

"What the hell are you doing? Can't you see I'm having a real moment? Don't you ever cut a scene when I'm having a real moment. What the fuck do you think I'm here for?"
TO *REBEL* DIRECTOR NICK RAY.

"Please lock me up . . . or I am going to do something."
DEAN'S MOST-QUOTED LINE: AS JIM STARK IN *REBEL WITHOUT A CAUSE*.

"Take it away, Limey. People will say 'James Dean can't even do his own stunts, he needs a mattress'."
REFUSING OFFER OF MATTRESS FROM PROP MAN TO FALL ONTO AS CARS GO OVER THE CLIFF EDGE IN *REBEL WITHOUT A CAUSE*.

"You look green — and you know how green photographs in colour."
TO NATALIE WOOD ON HER FIRST SCREEN KISS WITH HIM.

"Everything about Dean suggests the lonely, misunderstood 19-year-old. Even from a distance you know a lot about him from the way he walks — with his hands in his pockets and head down, slinking like a dog waiting for a bone. When he talks, he stammers and pauses, uncertain of what he is trying to say . . . when he listens he is full of restless energy."
NEW YORK TRIBUNE'S WILLIAM ZINNSSER.

"I am still emotionally unable to watch reruns of *Rebel Without A Cause*. I still talk of Jimmy . . . still find myself thinking of him at odd moments."
CO-STAR SAL MINEO.

"Dean has succeeded in giving commercial viability to a film which would otherwise scarcely have qualified. His shortsighted stare prevents him from smiling and the smile drawn from him by dint of patient effort constitutes a victory. His powers of seduction are such that he can kill father and mother on the screen nightly with the full blessing of both art-house and popular audiences."
FILM-MAKER/REVIEWER FRANÇOIS TRUFFAUT, *CAHIERS DU CINÉMA*.

"He is that rare thing, a young actor who is a great actor, and the troubled eloquence with which he puts over the problems of misunderstood youth may lead to him being accepted by young audiences as a sort of symbol, re-experience the feeling of being lost, unwanted and different."
HOLLYWOOD REPORTER'S JACK MOFFIT.

"Perhaps the mental unrest of the characters in the story (*Rebel*) made him wary . . . I began to feel that this time it was not so much a matter of study and research as it was a definite and strong feeling that he, too, belonged partly to that portion of humanity that is lost, alone, confused."
ACTOR/CONFIDANT BILL BAST REACTING TO DEAN'S *REBEL* PERFORMANCE.

"He acts like a gypsy playing the top string of the violin. A quarter tone higher, a fraction louder and it would set the teeth on edge. That judgement is half the pleasure. And James Dean knows very well how far it is possible to go."
GEORGES BEAUME ON *REBEL WITHOUT A CAUSE*.

"It was an incredible experience. Something happened during the making of that picture (*Rebel*) for everybody. It wasn't just making a movie. It was as close to a spiritual experience as you can get. And Jimmy was the focus, the centre of it all. It all happened because of him."
ACTOR SAL MINEO, CO-STAR IN *REBEL WITHOUT A CAUSE*.

"*Rebel*'s appeal was obvious. We were watching the intense, doomed performance of a dead youth, a myth, the myth of those who would wish to see themselves dead without dying. Dean was dead, pre-dead, dead upon our discovery of him. His vivid presence projected a fathomless absence. It was *thrilling*."
JOY WILLIAMSON, *ESQUIRE*.

WITH NATALIE WOOD IN REBEL WITHOUT A CAUSE

James Dean In His Own Words

"Never has any acting job taken so much out of me. I put everything I had into that one, and I'm pleased with the general result. Any writer, musician, painter or actor will tell you that when they look back on their work they know it could be improved. But in the end you have to say okay, that's it, it's finished — it stands or falls as it is. I now regard Natalie (Wood), Nick (Ray) and Sal (Mineo) as co-workers; I regard them as friends . . . about the only friends I have in this town (Hollywood). And I hope we all work together again soon."

DEAN'S SPEECH ON FINISHING THE SHOOTING OF *REBEL*.

"He was always so inspiring, so patient and so kind. He didn't act as if he were a star at all. We have each other's suggestions and he was very critical of himself, never satisfied with his work. When he played a scene, he had the ability to make everyone else look great, too. He used to come on the set and watch the scenes even when he wasn't in them. He was that interested in the whole picture, and not just in his own part."

REBEL CO-STAR NATALIE WOOD.

"Rehearsing with him kept us all on our toes. Without warning, he'd throw in different lines and improvise through scenes. Frankly, I didn't know what all the fuss was about. Then I saw the screening and he was great. He was sitting just behind me and half a dozen times I turned around to look at him. He was giving that grin of his and almost blushing, looking down at the floor between his legs."

REBEL CO-STAR SAL MINEO.

"Jimmy was often accused of imitating Marlon Brando. The person I think they were both possibly under the influence of was (director Elia) Kazan. Any common mannerisms were Kazan."

ACTRESS NATALIE WOOD, CO-STAR IN *REBEL WITHOUT A CAUSE*.

"If I could have just one day when I wasn't all confused . . . I wasn't ashamed of everything. If I felt I belonged some place."

DEAN AS JIM STARK IN *REBEL*.

Giant

WITH ELIZABETH TAYLOR IN GIANT

"George Stevens for my money is the greatest director of them all — even greater than Kazan."

"That Stevens was born for the movies. He's so real, so unassuming, and he didn't miss a thing. We've got a wonderful script for this one. When it wants to Hollywood can accomplish tremendous things: this movie might be one of them. I sure hope so."

"Then there's George Stevens, the greatest of them all. I'm supposed to do *Giant* for him. This guy was born for the movies. So real, unassuming. You'll be talking to him thinking he missed the point and then — bang! — he has it."

"An actor should thoroughly understand the character he is portraying. There's no better way than trying to be that person in the house, away from the camera. I developed a program of understanding Jett Rink and doing the things he'd be likely to do. I didn't want any jarring notes in my characterisation. Jet was a victim of his position in life. I wanted to play him sympathetically."
FROM A WARNER BROTHERS PRESS RELEASE.

"Are you finished? Well, let me tell you something. I am not a machine. I may be working in a factory, but I'm not a machine. I stayed up all night Friday to do that scene. I prepared all night for the scene. I came in ready to work and you kept me sitting around all day. Do you realise I'm doing emotional memories? That I'm working with my senses — my sight, hearing, smell, touch? Can I tell you that every day you make me sit, there'll be two days next time? Then three, then four? You'll pay for it. And you're not going to stop me from working. Now let's get back to the set."
IN ARGUMENT WITH *GIANT* DIRECTOR GEORGE STEVENS.

"What are you doing in here at this time of night?"
"I live here with probably more rights than you have. Don't you know who I am? My name is James Dean!"
"I don't care who you are. Get off this lot immediately and don't come back unless you're working. My name is Jack Warner." (Filming *Giant* in Texas).
ON BEING DISCOVERED LIVING IN HIS DRESSING ROOM – A PRACTICE NOT ALLOWED BECAUSE OF INSURANCE RATES. JACK WARNER OWNED HIS FILM COMPANY, WARNER BROTHERS.

"Thank you, Ma'am, but I like it the way it is."
REJECTING AN OFFER TO WASH THE SHIRT HE'D BEEN WEARING ON SET FOR TWO WEEKS.

"It was an amazing experience to work in a scene with Jimmy. You could feel the part come alive, and he would actually become the character. His concentration was so complete . . ."

GIANT CO-STAR ELIZABETH TAYLOR.

"Great, help me in my work. Like this part of Jett Rink I play in *Giant*, I had tape recordings of fellows with Texan accents. The thing to do is not to exaggerate the drawl . . . get it just right."

DEAN DISCOVERS THE TAPE RECORDER.

"Take a good look at me. You may not get the chance again."

TO GIANT PHOTOGRAPHY DIRECTOR WILLIAM C. MELLOR.

"They were all wet-eyed, so it must have been good . . ."

REVIEWING HIS OWN PERFORMANCE AT THE GIANT RUSHES.
(THE SCENE HE WAS WATCHING WAS RE-DUBBED AFTER HIS
DEATH DUE TO HIS INDISTINCT SPEECH.)

"In front of the camera he had an instinct that was nearly uncanny. I don't recall ever working with anyone who has such a gift. He was in shadow and had to lift his head to the light. We explained how it should go and he seemed to plan it exactly right to the half-inch first time. He seemed to know how it should be, without rehearsal or anything."

DIRECTOR OF PHOTOGRAPHY ON GIANT, WILLIAM MELLOR.

"Before coming on set he used to warm up, like a fighter before a contest. He never stepped into camera range without first jumping into the air with his feet up under his chin or running at full speed around the set shrieking like a bird of prey."

ACTOR ROCK HUDSON, STAR OF GIANT.

"Sometimes he broke a scene down into so many bits and pieces I couldn't see the wood for the trees. I must admit that I sometimes underestimated him; and sometimes he overestimated the effect he thought he was getting. Then he might change his approach, do it quick — and if that didn't work we'd effect a compromise. All in all, it was a hell of a headache to work with him."

GEORGE STEVENS, DIRECTOR, GIANT.

"He was always pulling and hauling and he had developed this cultivated, designed, irresponsibility. 'It's tough on you,' he seemed to imply, 'but I've got to do it this way.' From the director's angle, that isn't the most delightful sort of person to work with."

GEORGE STEVENS, DIRECTOR, GIANT.

"He gave the impression of being completely natural and improvising as he went along. But no single detail was ever impromptu. He had everything figured out . . . an actor working on inspiration alone couldn't do this . . . he had his own approach to acting and it was something elusive that nobody else ever tried on the screen."

GEORGE STEVENS.

"We were the same age, just a year or so between us: like brother and sister really. Kidding all the time, whatever it was we were talking about. One felt he was a boy one had to take care of, but even that was probably his joke. I don't think he needed anything or anyone — except his acting."

ACTRESS ELIZABETH TAYLOR, CO-STAR, GIANT.

"I sat there for three days, made up and ready to work at nine o'clock every morning. By six o'clock I hadn't had a scene or a rehearsal. I sat there like a bump on a log watching that hog lumpy Rock Hudson making love to Liz Taylor. I'm not going to take it any more."

"When you're a young actor in Hollywood, everyone comes up to you and tells you how James Cagney played that scene in 1930, and how Humphrey Bogart did it in 1940. Dean just eliminated that in one gesture."

ACTOR DENNIS HOPPER, CO-STAR, GIANT.

"The whole time I worked with the man I never got a civil word out of him. He always seemed resentful about something."

ACTOR ROCK HUDSON, CO-STAR, GIANT.

"I can see him now, blinking behind his glasses after having been guilty of some preposterous bit of behaviour, and revealing by his very cast of defiance that he felt some sense of unworthiness."

GEORGE STEVENS, DIRECTOR, GIANT.

"Jimmy and I found we were a bit neurotic, and had to justify our neuroses by creating, getting the pain out and sharing it."

ACTOR DENNIS HOPPER, CO-STAR, GIANT.

"In every word and gesture there was a poetical presence. I used to feel that he was a disturbed boy, tremendously dedicated to some intangible beacon of his own — and neither he nor anyone else might ever know what it was."

GEORGE STEVENS.

"I didn't like Dean particularly. He was hard to be around. He hated (director) George Stevens, didn't think he was a good director and he was always angry and full of contempt. He never smiled. He was sulky and had no manners."

ACTOR ROCK HUDSON, CO-STAR, GIANT.

WITH EDNA FERBER ON SET OF GIANT

"He was the glorification of hatred and sickness. When he got success he was victimised by it. He was a hero to people who saw him only as a little waif when actually he was a pudding of hatred."
ELIA KAZAN.

"Jimmy hated the hostile, hated being so moody and violent – the very things that American kids worship him for being. Once Jimmy was introduced to a producer at the studio. The producer put out his hand to shake his but Jimmy ignored it, just threw a fistful of pennies on the ground and just walked away. Afterwards in the car Jimmy began to cry. 'Why do I do these things?' he sobbed. He was always sorry that he had done such unreasonable things, always trying to correct them."
STEWART STERN, AUTHOR, *REBEL WITHOUT A CAUSE*.

"Stu, I'd like you to do me a favour. If you ever find out why I acted the way I did today, please tell me."
TO STEWART STERN AFTER INSULTING WARNERS EXECUTIVE STEVE TRILLING BY SCATTERING A HANDFUL OF COINS AT HIS FEET.

"On location in Texas I noticed that photographers always kept watch on Jim, knowing that sooner or later he would reward them with a fine picture. Maybe silhouetted lithe and lean against a gold and buttermilk sky or perhaps fooling with a length of rope, making it loop and unloop itself as he talked."
GEORGE STEVENS.

"It was pretty clear to a lot of people, that when Jimmy finished *Rebel* he was sitting on top of the world and then Stevens is pulling it out from under him – and I mean it was a deliberate thing. I don't know why Stevens had it in for him so much except that Jimmy seemed to intimidate him, to cast a bad light on Stevens when they were working. But maybe Stevens was just responding to the way Jimmy rubbed some really sore spot in the man.
"I know Stevens was rude to Dean and brushed him aside so he started to booze a lot and he'd be late and he'd be sarcastic and he just started fucking off. Okay, so he was getting even."
ACTOR DENNIS HOPPER.

"It is the late James Dean who makes his malignant role the most tangy and corrosive in the film. Mr Dean plays this curious villain with a stylised spookiness – a sly sort of off-beat languor and slur of language – that concentrates spite. This is a haunting capstone to the brief career of Mr Dean."
TIME MAGAZINE REVIEW.

"James Dean, who was killed in a sports-car crash two weeks after his last scene in *Giant* was shot, in this film clearly shows for the first (and fatefully the last) time what his admirers always said he had – a streak of genius. He has caught the Texas accent to nasal perfection. In one scene with Carroll Baker . . . Dean is able to press an amazing array of subtleties into the mood of the moment to achieve what is certainly the finest piece of narrative acting seen on screen since Marlon Brando and Rod Steiger did their 'brother scene' in *On The Waterfront*."
NEW YORK TIMES ON *GIANT*.

"Dean is very effective as a boy groping for adjustment to people. As a farewell performance he leaves behind with this film genuine artistic regret for here was a talent which might have touched the heights."
VARIETY MAGAZINE.

"That's not where I want to go!"
TO ACTRESS/CONFIDANTE EARTHA KITT AFTER *GIANT*.

"Dammit, I know I'm a much better actor than what's being done with me at the moment. I'm being inhibited, I'm not able to exercise the full capacity of my abilities."
AFTER *GIANT*.

"Fun days are over. It's time to start being a man . . ."
TO FRIEND AFTER *GIANT*.

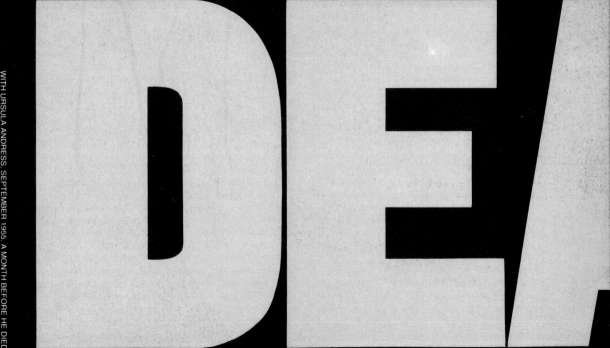

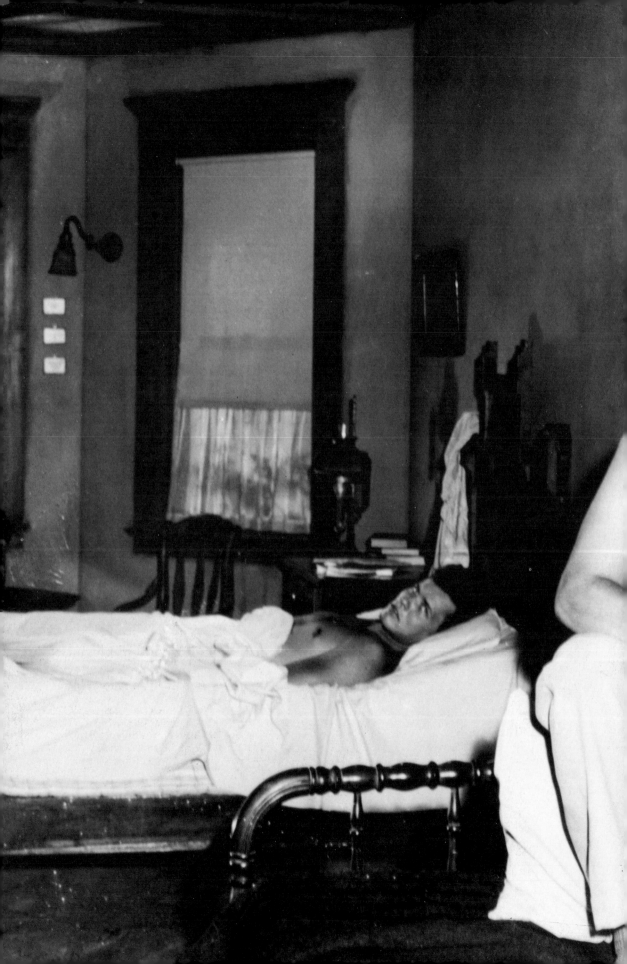

James Dean In His Own Words

"Jim had no time or energy for love. He wanted to save his emotions and his feelings for his work. I realised this and accepted it and tried to conceal my feelings."
ANONYMOUS CALIFORNIA UNIVERSITY STUDENT.

"He wasn't much to look at. He was too thin and short and probably the world's scruffiest dresser. But he was quite with it all. There was something about the way he cocked his hat that got me. He was dynamic and definite."
UNIDENTIFIED DATE (1).

"A girl gets the feeling that Jimmy, right away, is very sensitive and intelligent. He does not lead with the wise-cracks. He is natural, quiet. After a while he looks up at you and grins. It makes you feel very warm."
UNIDENTIFIED DATE (2).

"With all his crazy ways, he's the cutest guy we've had around Hollywood in a long long time. Problems or not, he's one boy we'd all like to hang on to."
UNIDENTIFIED ADMIRER.

"The best thing about being a bachelor is that you can get into bed from either side."

"I don't know. I go 'whoop' in the stomach when you ask if I'd like to meet her. Too much woman. You look at her and think 'I'd like to have *that*'."
DEAN ON MARLENE DIETRICH.

"I think that Jimmy died a virgin. He wasn't at all turned on by sex. He was very difficult to get to know. He kept very much to himself. At parties he would arrive late and disappear early and not mix at all."
ACTRESS CARROLL BAKER.

"What I remember most about Jimmy was his gentleness. Ours was a very private relationship. During the time we were together we saw as few other people as possible. It was the way both of us wanted it."
ACTRESS/SOMETIME GIRLFRIEND ELIZABETH 'DIZZY' SHERIDAN.

"You know, in Hollywood I see the most glamorous girls in the world. Expensive faces and bodies. But you're wholesome and like a good piece of bread to a hungry man. You're like sweet well water to a thirsty man."
TO BETTY LOU SIMMONS OF BATON ROUGE, LOUISIANA, ONE OF MANY ALLEGED CONQUESTS TO TALK AFTER HIS DEATH.

"Bought you a diamond ring and have placed order for 10, count them, 10 children. Stop. Miss you terribly and pray for you every night. Stop. Pray for me and love me. Jimmy."
TELEGRAM PURPORTEDLY RECEIVED BY SAME MISS SIMMONS ON THE EVE OF HIS DEATH, AS RECOUNTED TO *LOWDOWN* MAGAZINE.

James Dean In His Own Words

"You know, I think we ought to get married. Seriously, it would be so right to come home to somebody who understands me, who cares."
TO INSURANCE AGENT LEW BRACKER.

"Gay as a descriptive term would categorise Jimmy in such a limited manner. He tried a lot of new things and he was always open to new experiences, but I can't give an answer only because it would restrict rather than expand his personality. He was so many things . . ."
ACTOR/CONFIDANT BILL BAST.

"Well I'm certainly not going through life with one hand tied behind my back!"
ANSWER TO REPORTER ABOUT HIS ALLEGED BISEXUALITY.

"You can't draft me, I'm homosexual."
ALLEGED BY EX-FAIRMOUNT SELECTIVE SERVICE OFFICIAL AND A NOTED HOLLYWOOD FRIEND AS DEAN'S REASON GIVEN FOR HIS EXEMPTION FROM THE DRAFT.

"Nothing complicated, just a nice girl for a change. I mean, you know, I can talk to her. She understands. Nothing messy, just an easy kind of friendly thing. I respect her. She's untouchable. We're members of totally different castes. You know, she's the kind of girl you put on a shelf and look at. Anyway, her old lady doesn't like me. Can't say I blame her."
ON PIER ANGELI.

"Jimmy is a wonderful boy, a great actor. But we are very young, he will soon be 24. This is the first year I am allowed to go out alone. There is a very old joke in Hollywood that if a boy dates me he must also date my mother, my two sisters, my dogs and my parakeets. This is not true any more."
PIER ANGELI.

"He was the love of my youth — perhaps my greatest love."
PIER ANGELI LATER IN LIFE.

"She's so different from all the rest of the dolls I've seen in pictures. She's young, but she's got depth and philosophy."
ON PIER ANGELI.

"When in Rome, do as the Romans do. Welcome to Hollywood . . ."
TO MOTHER OF THEN-GIRLFRIEND PIER ANGELI WHEN TAKING HER HOME LATE.

"A lot of people have asked me about Pier Angeli. Well I met her when she was making *The Silver Chalice* and I was about to be in *Eden*. She's a rare girl. Unlike most Hollywood girls, Pier is real and genuine . . . and though she's young she has a rare insight into life. The only trouble is, she gets confused by listening to too many people."

"We used to go to the California coast and stay there secretly in a cottage on the beach. We would talk about ourselves and our problems about the movies and acting, about life and life after death. We were like kids together and that's the way we both liked it . . . it was all so innocent and emphatic."
ACTRESS/GIRLFRIEND PIER ANGELI TO THE *NATIONAL ENQUIRER*.

"For better or for worse, I'm going to spend the rest of my days with her."
TO ACTOR RICHARD DAVALOS ABOUT PIER ANGELI.

"Oh no . . . please say you're kidding me."
TO PIER ANGELI ON HER ANNOUNCEMENT OF THEIR BREAKUP.

"Things were different between us when I got back from New York. I kept asking Pier if there was someone else but she wouldn't tell me. Then, the night before her engagement was announced, she told me she was going to marry Vic Damone. I couldn't believe it."

"I was only in love once in my life, and that was with Jimmy Dean."
PIER ANGELI, IN LATER LETTER TO FRIEND.

"I wouldn't marry unless I could take care of a wife properly — and I don't think I'm emotionally stable enough to do that right now."

"He would run into a new face and attach himself to her for a few hours — or, at the most, a day. The girls would accompany him wherever he went: to his agent's office, on interviews, to rehearsals, to dinner, on walks or to his room."
ACTOR/CONFIDANT BILL BAST.

"Foreign girls intrigue me . . ."
ON DATING ACTRESS LESLIE CARON.

"Towards the end of *Giant* he really cut off all private relationships . . . except for Ursula Andress while *that* lasted. He was withdrawn and largely self-sufficient, his new home in the San Fernando valley was known around Hollywood as his Sanctuary of Isolation."
ACTRESS MAILA NURMI.

"I have never taken Vampira out, and I should like to clear this up. I have a fairly adequate knowledge of Satanic forces and I was interested to find out if this girl was obsessed by such a force. She was a subject about which I wanted to learn. I met her and engaged her in conversation. She knew absolutely nothing! She uses her inane characterisation as an excuse for the most infantile expressions you can imagine . . ."
ON ACTRESS MAILA NURMI, VAMPIRA ON TV.

"I don't go out with witches — and I dig dating cartoons even less."
TO HEDDA HOPPER, REFUTING ROMANCE WITH MAILA NURMI (VAMPIRA).

"He explained to me what happened with Pier. He said her family objected to him, and all the time they would have to sneak around to see each other. He found it was more of a joke with her — exciting because nobody was to know. When Pier stopped seeing him and began going out with Vic (Damone), Jimmy was hurt."

ACTRESS/GIRLFRIEND URSULA ANDRESS.

"It'd be cheaper to have a family. It's costing me five dollars every time I take you out. Why can't you eat spaghetti for 65 cents?"

TO URSULA ANDRESS AND HER GERMAN SHEPHERD DOG.

"We fight like cats and dogs — no, on second thoughts, like two monsters. But then we make up and it's fun. Ursula doesn't take any baloney from me and I don't take any baloney from her. I guess it's because we're both so egotistical."

ON URSULA ANDRESS.

"He came by my house late. He came in the room like a wild animal, and smelling of everything I don't like. We go hear jazz music and he leave table: says he go play drums. He no come back. I don't like to be alone. I go home. He come by my home later and say sorry. Ask I want to see his motorcycle. We sit on sidewalk in front of motorcycle and talk, talk, talk until five."

ACTRESS/GIRLFRIEND URSULA ANDRESS, 1955.

"He needed desperately someone to understand him. I tried to help and love him but it didn't work."

ACTRESS/GIRLFRIEND URSULA ANDRESS.

"They said I broke Jimmy's heart by ending our romance, that I sent him to his death in his sports car after he phoned me for the last time.

"They say Paramount ended my contract because of the crash. After saying I was a young Bergman they just dropped me. Nobody tells me why officially.

"I don't think Jimmy was ready for marriage. Once he said we should marry and visit my family in Switzerland. We were too much alike. We'd fight over nothing, yet we liked the same things . . .

"I think it must just have been his time on earth. I'm a fatalist. All of us have our time."

URSULA ANDRESS TO THE *SUNDAY CHRONICLE*.

"What the hell would she have in common with a poor farm boy? If it weren't that I was up there on the screen, her and people like her wouldn't give me the time of day."

ON URSULA ANDRESS.

"Jimmy made life hell for any girl who gave him affection. He was sick and unhealthy in attitude."

EAST OF EDEN DIRECTOR ELIA KAZAN.

"A woman knows when a man is not judging her by her physical appearance alone. She can see it in his eyes. That's why I liked Jimmy and is, I'm sure, why it was so easy for women to like him. The night they told me that Jimmy had died I knew that life would always be a little lonesome without him.

"I had letters wanting me to explain what our relationship was. My goodness, I couldn't possibly do that!"

ACTRESS/SOMETIME GIRLFRIEND LILI KARDELL.

"I haven't written because I've fallen in love. It had to happen sooner or later. It's not a very good picture of him but that's Cisco The Kid, the new member of the family. He gives me confidence. He makes my hands strong. May use him in the movie . . ."

TO ACTRESS/SOMETIME GIRLFRIEND BARBARA GLENN ON A THOROUGHBRED PALOMINO HORSE HE BOUGHT WHILE IN HOLLYWOOD.

WITH CO-STAR PAT HARDY, IN TV DRAMA THE UNLIGHTED ROAD, MAY 1955

"I have married a machine."
ON TAKING DELIVERY OF HIS FIRST RACER.

"A new addition has been added to the Dean family. I got a red '53 MG (milled head etc, hot engine). My sex pours itself into fat curves, broadslides and broodings, drags, etc. You have plenty of competition. My motorcycle, my MG and my girl. I have been sleeping with my MG. We make it together, honey."
LETTER TO ACTRESS/SOMETIME GIRLFRIEND BARBARA GLENN.

"I could never get along without my little cycle. I guess I'll never sell it. It's like a brother to me."
LETTER HOME FROM CALIFORNIA.

"I'll never sell this one. It's like a friend. And friends are hard to find in the theatre."
ON RECLAIMING A BIKE RIDDEN ON THE FARM.

"Now it's all over and we don't have to bug each other no more. And I can go back to my motor racing."
TO GIANT DIRECTOR GEORGE STEVENS.

"There isn't a single person you can't learn from. Like with the Porsche — I want to know as much as Rolf (mechanic Rolf Wutherich). I want to be able to do what he can, because I don't want to have to depend on him."

"Out on the track, I learn about people and myself."

"The odds were against his becoming a great racer. Dean was always too careful with other drivers. He didn't care about his own neck, but he wouldn't take any risks involving another driver. You can't win races that way.
   "Jimmy wanted speed, as a man wants a woman. He wanted his body to hurtle over the ground, the faster the better. He was a straightaway driver: his track was the shortest distance between here and there."
FELLOW RACING DRIVER KEN MILES.

"The road is no place to race your car. It's real murder. Remember — the life you save may be mine."
ROAD SAFETY TV CAMPAIGN WITH GIG YOUNG, 1955.

"Racing is the only time I feel whole."

"They sort of shoot around it . . . but they've never said 'Don't do it.' Everybody likes a winner, and so far I've been winning."
TO REPORTER ABOUT WARNERS' ATTITUDE TO RACING.

"Your profile resembles that of John Barrymore . . . but then your automobile racing will probably soon take care of that."
GIANT AUTHOR EDNA FURBER.

"An actor with half a face is no actor at all."
ACTOR MARLON BRANDO TO DEAN AT A PARTY. DEAN SOLD THE BIKE . . . BUT BOUGHT A CAR.

"I want to enter at Salinas, Willow Springs, Palm Springs — all the other places. Of course, I'll miss some of them because I have to do a TV spectacular in New York on October 18. But maybe I can catch a race back there.
   "When a man goes home at night, the studio can't tell him not to do what he wants to do. This is strictly a racing car, it goes like a bomb. I'll be very hard to catch."
TO REPORTERS, SEPTEMBER 16, 1955.

"When he told me the speed he wanted to go in (the Porsche) I begged him never to get into it. Something made me say, 'If you do, you will be dead in a week'."
SIR ALEC GUINNESS, SEPTEMBER 23, 1955 AT VILLA CAPRI.

"So long . . . I think I'll let the Spyder out . . ."
TO GEORGE STEVENS ON LEAVING GIANT SET IN HIS CAR.

"How do you like the Spyder now? I want to keep this car for a long time — a real long time."
TO COMPANION SANFORD ROTH.

"Before I can get in there and drive I've got to unlimber. I've got to be right for it."

"No one expected Dean to go like he did. He went out and left everybody. He was really blasting, going like a bomb. Sometimes he seemed to be smiling as he chased the car in front, overtook some and made for the leaders. He drove with his head lowered, his foot hard down on the accelerator, lost in the bright fever of the race as he so often lost himself in the bright fever of a role. He overtook the leader: no one could catch him now . . ."
REPORT OF HIS FIRST RACE AT PALM SPRINGS IN THE PORSCHE. FIRST IN THE AMATEUR RACE, HE WAS THEN THIRD IN THE PROFESSIONAL.

James Dean In His Own Words

"I never saw Jimmy as happy. He was singing and whistling and never stopped talking about the things he was going to do with that new car."
AN UNNAMED FRIEND.

"Come on, let's drive — it will blow the cobwebs right out of our heads, and man do I need that!"
TO ACTOR/CONFIDANT BILL BAST WHILE FILMING *EAST OF EDEN*.

"I plan to become World Racing Champion!"
DEAN TO MECHANIC ROLF WUTHERICH.

"With a car like this, who wants to be shut in that old bus?"
DEAN INDICATING FORD CAR, SEPTEMBER 30, 1955.

"I can't get it to run properly under 80 miles-per-hour . . ."
DEAN TO POLICEMAN HANDING HIM A TICKET FOR DOING 70 IN A 45 MILE-PER-HOUR ZONE.

"Man, I wish she'd lived to see all this. You know, she would only be 46 now."
ON THE ROAD TO HIS DEATH, TO MECHANIC ROLF WUTHERICH.

"Jimmy was a terribly destructive person. Our relationship was destructive. I knew he would destroy himself in the end and that's why when it came it wasn't a surprise; it was as though my reaction to it had happened long before. From the first time I met Jimmy I felt it. Whenever I waited for him I always wondered, 'Is he going to make it?'

"He bought a new bike and said, 'I'm going to go home'. It was winter. 'How?' I said. 'Please, if you're going to die, why don't you do it around here?' 'No I've got to try it. It's great . . . don't worry.'

"So Jimmy went to Indiana and I didn't hear from him for a couple of weeks. He went through snowstorms and through the ice and practically froze to death, but drove all the way out and back."
ACTRESS/ONE-TIME GIRLFRIEND BARBARA GLENN.

"See you in Pasa Robles . . ."
LAST WORDS TO COMPANION SANFORD ROTH.

"If you don't take it slower, you'll never reach Salinas alive."
POLICE PATROLMAN WHO GAVE DEAN A SPEEDING TICKET MINUTES BEFORE HIS DEATH.

DEA

"If I live to be a hundred, there won't be time to do everything I want."

"My mother died on me when I was nine-years-old. What did she expect me to do? Do it all myself?"
TO BROADCASTER WALLY ATKINSON.

"You know, Grandpa, in the movie *East Of Eden* it was so funny, 'cause I played a character called Cal . . . and Cal Dean, he was your father, right? Markie and I went to the cemetery today and saw where great granddaddy Cal Dean is buried. What was he like? Did he have any interest in art or anything? What kind of kid was he?"
QUESTIONING HIS GRANDFATHER ON HIS ANCESTRY.

"Do you realise that if you sleep eight hours a day, you have slept for 25 years by the time you're 75? There's not much difference being asleep and being dead, so you might as well say you've been dead for 25 years!"

"If a man can bridge the gap between life and death, I mean if he can live on after he dies, then maybe he was a great man."

"The crash itself was nothing. I felt no shock. No hurt . . . I could see myself lying there looking down on that other person who was Jimmy Dean and yet wasn't . . . I watched with amazement and wonder, and the realisation gradually sank over me — this is what we call death. But it wasn't 'Death' . . . the other body that lay down there was only a shell. I, the real I who had inhabited it, was still alive . . ."
EXCERPT FROM *JAMES DEAN RETURNS!* (READ *HIS OWN WORDS FROM THE BEYOND*).

"I worried too much about him. You know what a crazy life I lead. I just figured you never know . . . I might go out one night and never come home. Then what would happen to Marcus?"
GIVING AWAY A SIAMESE CAT PRESENTED TO HIM BY LIZ TAYLOR, JUST BEFORE HIS DEATH.

"What is the thing you respect above all else? That's easy. Death. It's the only thing left to respect. It's the one inevitable, undeniable truth. Everything else can be questioned. But death is truth. In it lies the only nobility for man, and beyond it the only hope."

"You know something? I never figured I'd like to see 18. Isn't that dumb? Each day I'd look in the mirror and say 'What, you still here?'"

"They gave me the creeps. They were all about death and dying, poems and things he just made up. They were his ideas on what it might be like to die, and how it would feel to be in the grave and all that."
PHOTOGRAPHER FRANK WORTH ON A VISIT TO DEAN'S HOUSE, SEPTEMBER 1955.

"His behaviour and personality seemed to be part of a pattern which invariably had to lead to something destructive. I always had a strange feeling that there was in Jimmy a sort of doomed quality."
LEE STRASBERG.

"Well, (Bob) Francis makes two . . ."
"Don't worry — I'll be the third!"
DEAN TO FRIEND REPORTING THE SECOND MUTUAL FRIEND TO BE INVOLVED IN AN AUTO ACCIDENT.

"You can't do the things I'm doing. I can flirt with death and come through."
TO PHOTOGRAPHER WHO TOTALLED HIS CAR AFTER FOLLOWING DEAN.

"The studio says I'm going to kill myself. Can you figure that? What do you think? I think it's great . . . doing this article for *Photoplay* and it's got a picture with me sitting on the speedster and it says the studio says 'This crazy kid's going to kill himself' . . ."
TO ACQUAINTANCE JOHN GILMORE.

"The creepiest thing about it was that, with the lid shut, it squashes your nose."
LYING IN A COFFIN FOR A DENNIS STOCK PHOTO SESSION, 1955.

"These bored looking people have me in a coffin — but it's small, more like it was made for a little child. A couple of times I've just stopped what I'm doing . . . the oxygen chases it away."
DESCRIBING A RECURRING DREAM THAT HE HAD DIED DURING *REBEL* TO JOHN GILMORE.

"If only I could accomplish something before I die."
TO ACTRESS/GIRLFRIEND BEVERLY WILLS AFTER NIGHTMARES, 1951.

"One crowded hour of glorious life is worth an age without a name. That's what I want to put on my tombstone. Can't you see it? That's what I want it to say! Tell Jack Warner . . ."
AT GOOGIES COFFEE SHOP ON SUNSET STRIP, QUOTING FIRST WORLD WAR POET ALAN SEEGER.

"If only he'd fallen off his bike as a kid, things might have been different. Trouble is, Jimmy never got hurt on that cycle. Maybe if he'd had just one fall, he'd have learned to be afraid."
UNCLE MARCUS WINSLOW.

"You know there's so much bread coming in I'd better make a will . . . I'll sit down one evening next week and do it properly. A few days won't matter: I don't feel ill or anything."

"I want 80 thousand dollars to go to my aunt and uncle Ortense and Marcus Winslow who raised me, a separate 10 thousand dollars for my grandparents Mr and Mrs Dean: also a separate 10 thousand dollars put by for young Marky's education. That's it, simple: nothing for no one else."
TO INSURANCE AGENT LOU BRACKER. THE WILL WAS NEVER SIGNED: DEAN'S FATHER INHERITED.

"I saw him on that last day. He was looking good, in high spirits, and that's why I'll never go for the suicide theory. I know, too, that we parted friends."
FATHER WINTON DEAN.

"That guy up there has got to stop, he's seen us . . ."
DEAN'S REPORTED LAST WORDS.

"Live fast, die young and leave a good looking corpse."

"You were too fast to live, too young to die . . ."
THE EAGLES

"The career of James Dean has not ended. It has just begun. And God himself is directing the production."
PASTOR XEN HARVEY AT DEAN'S FUNERAL.

"You would have thought that a boy being gone all these years would leave us in peace. But on Jimmy's birthday last year I looked out of the window and counted over a dozen cars parked outside the gate."
UNCLE MARCUS WINSLOW.

James Dean In His Own Words

"James Dean worshipped and reached for immortality. He got what he wanted . . ."
SINGER MORRISSEY, LATE OF THE SMITHS.

"I can understand his appeal. He played the role that helped rebellious young people to identify with him . . . When I delivered my sermon on that day 25 years ago, I told them that while we could bury his body, we could not bury his spirit. I had no idea I was being so prophetic. Jimmy's influence just grew and grew, and it's very evident that people feel him as a living presence today."
PASTOR XEN HARVEY, 1980.

"The night he was killed I was having dinner with a lot of his friends — Sal Mineo, Dick Davalos, Nick Adams. We were talking about Jimmy's lifestyle and Nick ventured the opinion that Jimmy wouldn't live till 30. We pooh-poohed the idea. Later, when we finished eating, Nick and Sal walked me to my hotel. I was still under age then, with a studio chaperone, and it was she who heard the news.

"She told Nick and Sal and asked them not to say anything to me because I had an early call the next day and she wanted me to sleep. So they left rather abruptly. Next morning, the chaperone had to tell me because down in the lobby the newspapers had it all on the headlines. I didn't believe it. I think I stood at the window staring out for a long time. I went to work in a state of shock."
NATALIE WOOD.

"Suddenly the phone rang. I heard him (George Stevens) say 'No. My God. Are you sure?' and he kind of grunted a couple of times and hung up the phone. He stopped the film and turned on the lights and stood up and said to the room 'I've just been given the news that Jimmy Dean has been killed.'

"There was an intake of breath. No one said anything. I couldn't believe it . . . none of us could. Several of us started calling newspapers, hospitals, the police, the morgue . . .

"After maybe two hours the word was confirmed. Then everybody drifted out to their cars to go home. It was about nine o'clock at night: the studio was deserted. As I walked to my car feeling numb, I saw a figure coming through the lights down one of the little side streets. It was George getting into his Mercedes. We looked at each other and I said, 'I can't believe it George, I can't believe it.' And he said, 'I believe it. He had it coming to him, the way he drove. He had it coming to him'."
ELIZABETH TAYLOR.

WITH ELIZABETH TAYLOR DURING MAKING OF GIANT

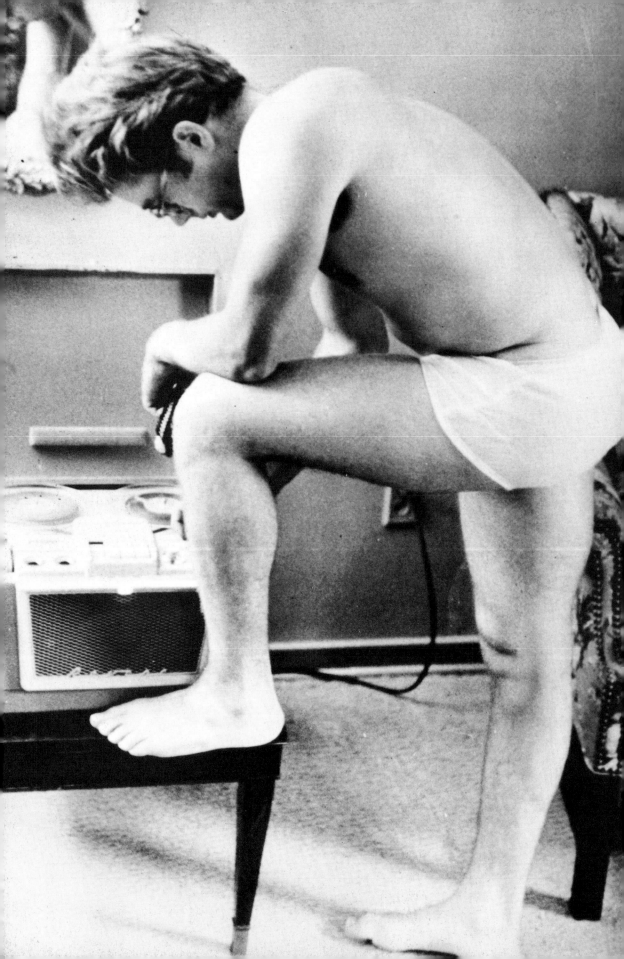

The Things They Said . . . About Jimmy

"I always envied Jimmy. My Dad never took time to play with me, but (Uncle) Marcus was forever out there shooting baskets with him or passing a football or taking him hunting or showing him how to do stunts."
A SCHOOL CLASSMATE.

"He was always polite and thoughtful; his enthusiasm for everything that pertained to the theatre was boundless. One day in class Jimmy read some scenes from Edgar Allan Poe's *Telltale Heart*. He was magnificent — but then he always had a spectacular emotion for any scene he played. Later, during that same class, I asked Jimmy to read some scenes from *Hamlet*. That night when I returned home I informed my husband that I had finally found the right student to play *Hamlet* as I felt it should be played."
JEAN OWEN, DRAMA TEACHER AT SANTA MONICA CITY COLLEGE TO *MOVIELAND* MAGAZINE.

"He was shy and awkward peering through big horn-rimmed glasses at a world that baffled him. One evening a boy I had dated invited him to join our crowd for a beer at The Point, a small café overlooking the Pacific where the younger crowd could go to drink beer, look at the ocean, and talk. But Jimmy wasn't in the talking mood that evening. He contented himself with watching the waves breaking on the shore. He had no use for small talk."
FELLOW COLLEGE STUDENT IN *PICTURE POST*.

"The unobtrusive young man with the unruly, sandy-coloured hair quietly roamed the campus apparently minding his own business and only occasionally projecting himself beyond the shell-rims of his thick-lensed glasses. He appeared to be nothing more than a simple, withdrawn little boy, not too long off the farm."
ACTOR/CONFIDANT BILL BAST.

"On weekends when he could afford it he went to Tijuana, Mexico, to see the bullfights. Bullfighting fascinated him for a while, and he practised cape movements at home to the accompaniment of appropriate Spanish music."
ACTOR/CONFIDANT BILL BAST.

"All adolescents want to rope steers . . . and sculpt busts of famous novelists and drive a custom sports car and write poetry and be a great Hollywood star. Dean did it . . . in a way, the kids feel he did it all for them."
MARTIN MAYER, *ESQUIRE*.

"Every boy goes through a period when he's 17 or so when he hates his father, hates authority, can't live within the rules . . . It's a classic case. Dean just never got out of it."
ELIA KAZAN, DIRECTOR, *EAST OF EDEN*.

"When I was a young actor in New York there was a saying that if Marlon Brando changed the way actors acted, James Dean changed the way people lived. I believe that. No one came before him and there hasn't been anyone since."
ACTOR MARTIN SHEEN.

"In Hollywood, where actors were picked, plucked and packed away, Dean was determined to make it on his own terms . . . it was rumoured, far too frequently, that he had worked his way up trousers down."
SINGER MORRISSEY, LATE OF THE SMITHS.

"When Jimmy posed in the driveway of his aunt and uncle's house, he'd already written the caption for the picture: 'You can't go home again'."
PHOTOGRAPHER DENNIS STOCK ON A RETURN TRIP TO FAIRMOUNT.

"Between belief and action lay the obstacle of Jimmy's deep, obscure uncertainty. Disappointed or unsatisfied, he was the child who goes to his private corner and refuses to speak."
NICK RAY, DIRECTOR, *REBEL WITHOUT A CAUSE*.

"Jimmy didn't know how to take hard criticism. He had no acting persona that could soak it up and deal with it and not let it get through to him too personally. It just bewildered him. Then he'd have to sort himself out before he could sort out what was wrong in the acting."
DICK DAVALOS (ARON IN *EAST OF EDEN*).

"Maybe he used his sometimes perverted humour to hide a sense of morality that most people would misunderstand. Jimmy had a high sense of morality — high in the sense that there was no pressure coming from anywhere. It was all inner, but it was very strong."
ACTOR BILL GUNN.

"You'll notice in many pictures that he's got his left cheek resting in his hand. There seems to be this constant reaching up to his own face, as if one side of it was slipping down or collapsing . . ."
SCULPTOR KENNETH KENDALL, WHOSE BUST OF DEAN ONCE SAT IN FAIRMOUNT CEMETERY.

"He felt he was being sacrificed for Taylor and Rock Hudson and he was not pleased about it. He blamed everything on the director. He said the picture *(Giant)* was going too big in an artificial way. He wanted the interpretation of him as an old man to be quite different from what it was turning out to be."
ACTRESS/CONFIDANTE EARTHA KITT.

James Dean In His Own Words

"He hugged me and kissed me as he always did, but I couldn't feel him . . . it was the strangest sensation. I said 'What's the matter with you? I don't feel you.' And he said, 'Kitt, you're being a witch again'."
ACTRESS/CONFIDANTE EARTHA KITT.

"He didn't comb his hair. He had a safety pin holding his pants together. He was introspective and very shy."
ACTRESS NATALIE WOOD.

"When I worked with him on TV, I found him to be an intelligent young actor who seemed to live only for his work. He was completely dedicated and, although a shy person, he could hold a good conversation on many wide-ranging topics."
ACTOR (!) RONALD REAGAN.

"For a moment we sat talking, and finally I got scared and told him I wouldn't go. 'You drive too fast, Jimmy,' I said. 'I got to,' he said. 'I'm not going to be around very long'."
BEVERLY LONG, CO-STAR IN *REBEL WITHOUT A CAUSE*.

"I had seen him driving in another race — he hadn't been racing long, but he was a good driver: he had that essential feel for fast cars and dangerous roads. He had that sixth sense a racing driver can't do without. We talked about his car for a couple of minutes, and then he took off . . . for a win. Two weeks later I was walking along Hollywood Boulevard when I saw Jimmy Dean coming towards me . . ."
AUTO MECHANIC ROLF WUTHERICH.

"I taught Jimmy to believe in personal immortality. He had no fear of death. He believed as I do that death is merely a control of mind over matter."
FAIRMOUNT MINISTER JAMES DEWEERD, AN INFLUENCE ON THE YOUNG DEAN.

"There was something suicidal in his nature, but I don't think it was a conscious thing."
ACTRESS CARROLL BAKER.

"Dean was never a friend of mine, but he had an *idée fixe* about me. Whatever I did, he did. He was always trying to get close to me. He used to call up. I'd listen to him talking to the answering service, asking for me, leaving messages. But I never spoke up. I never called him back."
ACTOR MARLON BRANDO.

"He was never a friend of mine . . . I hardly knew him. (But) he was always trying to get close to me. I finally met him at a party where he was throwing his weight around, acting the madman. So I spoke to him. I took him aside and asked him didn't he know he was sick? That he needed help . . . he listened to me. He knew he was sick. I gave him the name of an analyst and he went. And at least his work improved. Towards the end I think he was beginning to find his own way as an actor."
ACTOR MARLON BRANDO.

"Mr Dean appears to be wearing my last year's wardrobe and using my last year's talent . . ."
MARLON BRANDO.

"Why not wear something else besides last year's suits?"
BRANDO TO DEAN.

"I got the impression he felt awkward in others' company. I think in some ways he was an unloved child and that affected his judgement of people. There hadn't been any way to turn that insecurity outwards so it had gone in and taken hold of his personality."
ACTRESS CARROLL BAKER.

"I remember one cold winter's day we'd been making music out on the streets for hours — me on guitar, Jimmy on bongos. We'd made about two dollars each. I said 'Let's split and get some food.' I spent the money on a hot coffee, he spent his on seeing a movie."
MOONDOG, NEW YORK STREET SINGER.

"I thought he was pretty much of a creep until we got to the picnic and then all of a sudden he came to life. We began to talk about acting and Jimmy lit up. He told me how interested he was in the Stansilavsky method where you not only act people but things too.

"'Look,' said Jimmy, 'I'm a pine tree in a storm.' He held his arms out and waved wildly. To feel more free, he impatiently tossed off his cheap, tight blue jacket. He looked bigger as soon as he did because you could see his broad shoulders and powerful build. Then he got wilder and pretended he was a monkey. He climbed a big tree and swung from a high branch. Dropping from the branch he landed on his hands like a little boy, chuckling uproariously at every little thing. Once in the spotlight, he ate it up and had us all in stitches all afternoon. The 'creep' had turned into the hit of the party."
BEVERLY WILLS, YOUNG ACTRESS COURTED BY DEAN, TO *MODERN SCREEN* MAGAZINE SIX YEARS LATER.

EARTHA KITT

James Dean In His Own Words

"He wanted to do everything for us, buy us presents — just keep us. Any bills we had we would pay. We were young and had our own careers and our pride and we couldn't handle it. Jimmy had our love anyway — he didn't have to start buying it."

ACTRESS/GIRLFRIEND ELIZABETH 'DIZZY' SHERIDAN, AFTER A RUN IN *SEE THE JAGUAR* LED TO PARTS IN TV PLAYS.

"James Dean has defined what might be called the panoply of adolescence, a wardrobe in which is expressed a whole attitude towards society. Blue jeans, heavy sweaters, leather jacket, no tie, unbuttoned shirt, deliberate sloppiness are so many ostensible signs . . . of a resistance against the social conventions of adults."

AUTHOR EDGAR MORIN.

"One Sunday evening I was on my way home and it was bad weather, rain. And he's there, in the doorway, waiting for me. I say 'Whatsa the matter with you. You crazy? It's rain! Look at you, wrinkled shirt. Whatsa the matter, you drunk?'

"So he came upstairs and I tried to give him some coffee, but he wouldn't take it. He kept looking at the time. Finally, he said, 'Look Pop I gotta go now, but I'll be back. You put this station on the TV and watch my show, okay?' So we all sit down and watch the television and about 15 minutes later, we see Jimmy on the screen, looking jest like he did when he was here. He played the part of a drunkard, some drunk man who had an accident or something. But it appeared so natural! He was jest like when he was here sitting with us. He'd been playing like he was drunk. I'd never seen him drunk before and I'd been a little worried about him. But he was playing drunk like he was drunk for TV.

"Then he came back in here and walked in laughing like hell. That's the way he liked to do things."

POPPA LUCCI, OWNER OF THE TAVERN WHERE DEAN ATE.

"Nothing Jimmy did was ever a sideline. He put everything into everything he did. In his photography he was constantly searching for the new, even the odd. Sometimes the results were bizarre. But it was always Jimmy."

PHOTOGRAPHER ROY SCHATT.

"His quest for artistic truths was frightening. He wanted to know just about every single fact, idea and theory that had been discovered by man clear back to the Stone Age. He was much too suspicious of people, but he has a tremendous respect for any who had knowledge."

PEGOT WAREING, SCULPTRESS.

"He was interesting because he was complex, a combination of good and bad. Sometimes he was very close to you, and at other times he could completely ignore you and pretend not to hear and act affected. You never knew if he liked you or not.

"He liked talking to and being with cowboys, farmers, bums — anyone from whom he could improve himself as an actor. In the beginning he studied from books, later his learning became instinctive. After *Eden* he seemed to have lost interest. He changed in that he only saw the phoney, ugly parts in people and had become very cutting in his remarks."

JACK GARFEIN, A FRIEND AND FILM DIRECTOR WHO KNEW HIM BEFORE HIS BIG BREAK.

"He sapped the minds of his friends as a bloodsucker saps the strength of an unsuspecting man. Almost fanatically, he approached each person he met, whether prominent or obscure, with the same attitude: 'I will draw from him all he knows'."

ACTOR/CONFIDANT BILL BAST.

"I think he didn't understand what he was all about. He was very frustrated because he felt there was something within himself that he didn't understand. He knew that he wanted to go some place and the place he wanted to go to — he didn't understand that either. And he was reaching for someone to help him find out whatever it was he wanted to reach . . ."

ACTRESS/CONFIDANTE EARTHA KITT.

"Jimmy became subject to more frequent periods of depression and would slip off into a silent mood at least once each day. If I had thought it difficult to communicate with him at other times in the past I had never known such lack of communication as existed during his fits of depression. He would sit in his room, sit there and stare into space for hours. I made several attempts to get through to him but rarely got more than a grunt or a distant stare as response."

ACTOR/CONFIDANT BILL BAST.

"I really don't understand why, after all these years and countless exhibits that included portraits of Marilyn Monroe, Paul Newman, Eve Marie Saint and many many more, the only photos that were ever stolen from the walls were those of James Dean. At one point I had lost so many that I put a quarter-inch plastic shield over the most popular 'Torn Sweater' shot. My effort was in vain. I don't know how someone managed to pry off the two six-inch screws, but they did. I've now stopped exhibiting his portraits."

ROY SCHATT, PHOTOGRAPHER AND DEAN'S TEACHER.

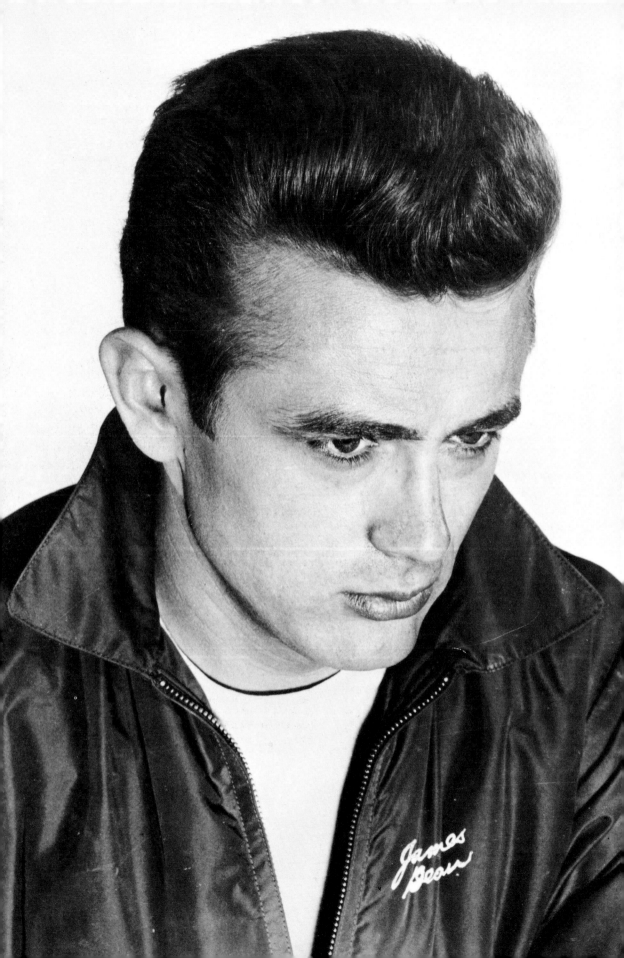

"There's a lot of jealousy about Jimmy in terms of why should he have all this admiration. Why should people have a kind of thing about him all these years after he's passed? Well, there's only two people in the world that I can remember in my lifetime creating that thing. One was Marilyn Monroe, and the other was James Dean."
SINGER/ACTOR SAMMY DAVIS JR.

"There was something about this guy. There was a strength, an assurance, a dedication and an independence. He had about him the air of a man who was quietly determined to grow, to develop, *never* to stop, *always* to go on trying."
ACTOR/CONFIDANT BILL BAST.

"Dean was a sentimental idealist striving for a world of perfection through a universal means of communication, love. Desperately he searched for that refuge where he could lay down his head without it being trampled on by disillusioners. On the other hand he was a rugged individualist, a realist in the basest sense of the word, ardently defending the right to exist in a manner that suited him, fervently refusing to relinquish even a portion of his right to do, be, feel or think whatever was natural to him.
   "When he saw sorrow he cried, or jeered bitterly at Power which had allowed it. When he saw humour, he laughed loud and hard; when he saw beauty he was peaceful and gentle; and when he saw himself he was sometimes puzzled, sometimes sickened."
ACTOR/CONFIDANT BILL BAST.

"Everyone respects him as a rebel and things, but he's an acceptable rebel. It's the same as Mick Jagger . . . they're both part of the establishment."
ADMAN PAUL WILSON OF THE J. WALTER THOMPSON AGENCY.

"The man knew where it was at, he was rockin' . . ."
MICK JAGGER.

"He was a genius. I don't think there's another actor in the world who could have portrayed Jet as well as he. But, like most geniuses, Dean then suffered from success poisoning. It's a common ailment with good actors and I'm glad to hear that his friends allowed him that much. He deserved it."
EDNA FURBER, AUTHOR, *GIANT*.

"People say he was unsure of himself. Yet he was certain of his direction as an actor, sure of his motive for being the way he was and doing the things he did. If he'd lived, he would have founded a school of acting here in Hollywood and become a great movie producer as well as a performer. He was only at the start of his big adventure. That is the *real* tragedy of his death."
ACTRESS NATALIE WOOD.

"James Dean is as much a controversial figure today (1964) as he was during his too brief life. He too was a victim of post-war America whose competitive economies and false values turned people into commodities . . . James Dean personified the rebels without causes searching for worthwhile identity. And like the age in which he lived he was restless, rootless and intensely curious about life. He was eager to succeed, eager to 'make it'. People sensed these qualities. They came through. The posthumous hysteria was authentic. The adulation is real. It comes from millions who recognised their own frustrations and understood them better because of Dean's search for his own identity."
DAVID DAVENPORT, SAN JOSE, CALIFORNIA, IN *SCREEN FACTS* MAGAZINE.

"In 16 months of acting, he left more of a lasting impression on the public than many stars do in 30 years. I can understand why the impact of his personality was so great. Though he was not an easy person to know, it was worth breaking his reserve. He was naturally shy and didn't like to make small talk. Once Jimmy felt he could trust a person he opened up. He was an exciting and stimulating person to be with. I believe he could be described as a genius."
HENRY GINSBURG, PRODUCER, *GIANT*.

"He'd hardly broken water, flashing in the air like a trout. A few more films and the fans wouldn't have been so bereft. This first bright phase would have become an ordinary light and would not have produced this kind of thing."
GEORGE STEVENS

"I haven't yet recovered from the tragic and untimely death of Jimmy Dean, one of the greatest talents I've come across for many a year. There were many here who thought he was impossible — but those who did never took the trouble to understand what made him tick. He would knuckle to no man, nor be a slave to any. But through understanding and affection he would do anything. His talent has been likened to that of Marlon Brando. I believe that, had he lived, he would have gone far ahead of Brando."
COLUMNIST HEDDA HOPPER.

James Dean In His Own Words

"To me, the clearest reason for his screen success was that the sense of intimacy, warmth and directness that he had on the screen came directly from his private life. That is, if that was the way he wanted it to be. He also could shut you off like a light."
ACTOR/CONFIDANT BILL BAST.

"Most of his newly found sophistication was becoming to him. Although a worldly way of thinking was completely new to him, he took it in his stride, even appearing blasé and unimpressed with all he was learning and all he was experiencing."
ACTOR/CONFIDANT BILL BAST.

"Before James Dean you were either a baby or a man. There was nothing in-between . . ."
ACTOR SAL MINEO (CO-STAR *REBEL WITHOUT A CAUSE*).

"A lot of people knew about him from his television work. The charisma was already working — and not just in his acting. Even if people didn't know who he was they'd turn and look at him walking down the street. I mean, *no one* walked like that in those days."
FILM DIRECTOR JOE MASSOT, 1953.

"It's impossible to speculate, but one thing's for certain — he would never have been ordinary. He was a one-off, I guess."
ACTRESS CARROLL BAKER.

"With his death we lost not only a movie star but a Hamlet, an Orestes, a Peer Gynt — that is, an actor who could *really* act."
HOWARD SACKLER.

"His death caused a loss in the movie world that our industry could ill afford. Had he lived long enough I feel he would have made some incredible films. He had sensitivity and the capacity to express emotion."
ACTOR GARY COOPER.

"I knew by heart all the dialogue of James Dean's films: I could watch *Rebel Without A Cause* a hundred times over."
ELVIS PRESLEY.

"I think Dean died at the right time. He would never have been able to keep up with all that publicity."
ACTOR HUMPHREY BOGART.

"America has known many rebellions but none like this. Millions of teenage rebels heading for nowhere some in hot rod cars, others on the blare of rock 'n' roll music, some with guns in their hands. And at their head a dead leader."
PICTURE POST, 1956.

"Dearest Jimmy, all this remembrance of you on your anniversary is a waste of time because I know you are still alive. Why worry so much about the way you look because your fans worship you no matter how disfigured you are."
FAN LETTER 1956, A YEAR AFTER HIS DEATH.

"The older generation had God. We have James Dean."
ANONYMOUS TEENAGE INTERVIEWEE IN 1957.

"Four years ago I had the feeling that he would be the biggest international property in the world. In licensing terms I thought it was another Snoopy, Garfield — a Mickey Mouse. And at that time there were no controls over the way the image was projected."
MARK ROESLER, ADVISOR/LAWYER TO THE DEAN FAMILY, 1987.

"The Dean legend is a sick legend which has been carried to morbid lengths. James would have been appalled."
STEWART STERN, WRITER OF *REBEL WITHOUT A CAUSE*.

ELVIS PRESLEY, 1956

Film And Dramatography

Feature motion pictures

Sailor Beware. Paramount 1951. Directed by
Hal Walker.
Starred Dean Martin, Jerry Lewis, Corinne
Calvert, Marion Marshall, Robert Strauss.
Dean had a bit part.

Fixed Bayonets. 20th Century Fox 1951.
Directed by Samuel Fuller.
Starred Richard Basehart, Gene Evans,
Michael O'Shea, Richard Hylton, Skip
Homeier.
Dean's one line ended up on the cutting room
floor.

Has Anybody Seen My Gal? Universal-
International 1952. Directed by Douglas Sirk.
Starred Charles Coburn, Piper Laurie, Lynn
Bari, Rock Hudson, Gigi Perreau, William
Reynolds, Larry Gates.
Dean played a customer in an ice cream
parlour.

East Of Eden. Warner Brothers 1955.
Directed by Elia Kazan. Screenplay by Paul
Osborn from John Steinbeck's novel.
Starred Julie Harris, Raymond Massey, Burl
Ives, Albert Dekker, Jo Van Vleet, Dick
Davalos.

Rebel Without A Cause. Warner Brothers
1955. Directed by Nicholas Ray. Screenplay
by Stewart Stern, from adaptation of story by
Nicholas Ray.
Starred Natalie Wood, Sal Mineo, Jim
Backus, Ann Doran, Rochelle Hudson,
William Hopper, Corey Allen.

Giant. Warner Brothers 1956. Directed by
George Stevens. Screenplay by Fred Guoil
and Ivan Moffat from Edna Ferber's novel.
Starred Elizabeth Taylor, Rock Hudson,
Carroll Baker, Dennis Hopper, Jane Withers,
Mercedes McCambridge, Chill Wills, Sal
Mineo, Rod Taylor, Earl Holliman.
Dean nominated Academy Award as best
actor.

The James Dean Story. Warner Brothers
1957. Directed by George W. George and
Robert Altman.
Narrated by Martin Gabel.

Television appearances

1951
Pepsi Cola commercial.
Father Payton's TV Theatre (*Hill Number
One,* an hour-long TV play directed by Jerry
Fairbanks).
Dean played John the Baptist.
Beat The Clock game show. Dean was warm-
up man.

1952
US Steel Hour (*Prologue To Glory*).

1953
Studio One Summer Theatre (*Sentence Of
Death*).
Danger (*No Room, Death Is My Neighbour,
The Little Woman*).
Campbell Sound Stage (*Something For An
Empty Briefcase*).
Kate Smith Hour (*The Hound Of Heaven*).
Lux Video Theatre (*Interview*).
Armstrong Circle Theatre (*The Bells Of
Cockaigne*).
Treasury Men In Action (*Case Of The
Watchful Dog, Case Of The Sawed-Off
Shotgun*).
Omnibus. *The Big Story.*
Kraft TV Theatre (*Keep Our Honor Bright, A
Long Time Till Dawn*).
Campbell Sound Stage (*Life Sentence*).
Johnsons Wax Programme (*Robert
Montgomery Presents Harvest*).

1954
Philco Playhouse (*Run Like A Thief*).
General Electric Theatre (*I Am A Fool, The
Dark Dark Hours*).
Danger (*Padlocks*).

1955
Schlitz Playhouse (*The Unlighted Road.
Dean plays a psychopath*).
US Steel Hour (*The Thief*).

Theatrical appearances on Broadway

1952
See The Jaguar. Directed by Michael Gordon.
Premièred at the Cort Theatre on December 3.
Starred Arthur Kennedy, Constance Ford,
Cameron Prud'homme, George Tyne,
Roy Fant.
Dean played Wally Wilkins.

1954
The Immoralist. Directed by Daniel Mann.
Premièred at the Royal Theatre on February 8.
Starred Louis Jourdan, Geraldine Page,
Charles Dingle, Paul Huber, Jon Heldabrand.
Dean played second lead as Bachir.

Radio work

1951
Bit parts in *Alias Jane Doe, Sam Spade, CBS
Radio Workshop, Stars Over Hollywood.*

James Dean In His Own Words

Mick St Michael

Omnibus Press
London/New York/Sydney

DEA

GIFT

© Copyright 1989 Omnibus Press
(A Division of Book Sales Limited)

Edited by Chris Charlesworth
Art Direction by Mike Bell
Book designed by Carroll, Dempsey & Thirkell
Picture Research by Debbie Dorman
Project and typesetting co-ordinated by Caroline Watson

ISBN 0.7119.1785.X
Order No: OP45301

Exclusive distributors:

Book Sales Limited,
8/9 Frith Street,
London W1V 5TZ, UK.

Music Sales Corporation,
225 Park Avenue South,
New York, NY 10003, USA.

Music Sales Pty Limited,
120 Rothschild Avenue,
Rosebery, NSW 2018, Australia.

To the Music Trade only:
Music Sales Limited,
8/9 Frith Street,
London W1V 5TZ, UK.

Picture credits:
Pictorial Press: p.4, 6, 8, 11, 14, 19, 20, 24, 26, 41, 42, 54, 56, 58, 63,
64, 68, 70, 74, 80, 81, 82, 89, 90, 94.
London Features International: p.12, 17, 23, 28, 31, 32, 34, 36, 39, 45,
46, 48, 57, 60, 66, 72, 76, 84, 87.

Every effort has been made to trace the copyright holders of the
photographs in this book but one or two were unreachable. We would
be grateful if the photographers concerned would contact us.

Typeset by Capital Setters, London.

Printed in England by Courier International Ltd, Tiptree, Essex.